GUIDEPOSTS
in Time of
CHANGE

The Lectures contained in this book were delivered at Amherst College in the winter of 1947–1948. They were made possible by a gift to the College from Charles E. Merrill of the Class of 1908.

GUIDEPOSTS
in Time of
CHANGE

Some Essentials for a Sound American Economy

By JOHN MAURICE CLARK

PROFESSOR OF ECONOMICS, COLUMBIA UNIVERSITY

Six Lectures
delivered at
Amherst College

HARPER & BROTHERS

NEW YORK

GUIDEPOSTS IN TIME OF CHANGE

C O N T E N T S

v

CHAPTER VI. COLLECTIVE BARGAINING AND WAGES

CHAPTER VII. CHANGING BALANCES: UNCOMMON REQUIREMENTS FOR THE COMMON MAN

The invitation to deliver six lectures on the Merrill Foundation at Amherst College, of which this small volume is the embodiment, reached me after completing the W. W. Cook lectures at the University of Michigan, now published under the title: "Alternative to Serfdom." If I had known at the time of the earlier lectures that Amherst was going to honor me with a second opportunity of a similar sort, the division of labor between the two series would probably have been different—perhaps it is idle to speculate whether it would have been better. As they stand, while each volume can be read as a unit, the two are complementary.

One thing that could not have been foreseen at the time of the earlier lectures was that Russian relations would have moved into a phase of openly-avowed crisis, making a frank public statement on this subject appropriate. This threat is clearly the first condition which a sound American economy has to meet. The thoughts here expressed on this theme have been long germinating, and can be regarded as having been substantially formulated in the summer of 1947, while public discussion was still in its early stages. Perhaps the best fate one could hope for them is that, by the time they appear in print, they may have become familiar commonplaces. It is too much to hope that they should have become obsolete by a resolving of the international *impasse*. The subject proved too large to dispose of in one lecture hour, and in the published version

I am making two chapters of it, so that six lectures become seven chapters.

Next comes putting our own house in order, the logical first step being to clarify our objectives. Here I have stressed what I have called the "principle of strategic decisions." It is, of course, merely common sense; but I have given it a weighty name in the hope of promoting its recognition as valid economic theory, in which capacity it might serve to combat some of the sterilizing pedantries that afflict some branches of that discipline.

The next three lectures move on to a more technical discussion of the economic mechanism, dealing with methods of sustaining the flow of purchasing, and attacking the stubborn problem of the effects of the structure of prices and wages on the total volume of production and employment. In particular, I have tried to formulate a theory of wages which might afford a basis for an economically sound wage policy.

In the concluding lecture, I have discussed some of the broader changes which mark the present and the coming era as a period of transition, which will tax our best capacities of adaptation. The one thing that is impossible is a return to past standards of "normalcy."

Finally, I must express my profound gratitude to those in charge of the Merrill Foundation, for the opportunity to return to Amherst in a new capacity, renewing old friendships, and for the challenge, uncomfortable as it was at times, to try to think through difficult problems and to formulate the results in terms accessible to a wider public than professional economists, so far as might be done without sacrifice of substance. The effort, at least, has been rewarding.

J. M. CLARK

New York City
September 1, 1948

GUIDEPOSTS
in Time of
CHANGE

THE TOTALITARIAN THREAT

1. FACING THE TASK OF PEACE, WITHOUT ILLUSIONS

At present, our system has one top priority purpose which is "obvious and simple": namely, self-preservation against the totalitarian threat, at present embodied in Soviet Russia. For a sound American society, this is the first requirement; and that is my excuse for speaking about it, not any claim to special knowledge about Russia. In presenting this threat, I conceive it to be a duty to promote understanding, in the service of peace. But "understanding" calls for courageous fact facing; it is not synonymous with "glossing over," still less with "appeasement." And the kind of peace that is tolerable to us is peace by voluntary action, not by submission to world conquering dictatorship. So it is our duty to search with special earnestness for factors on which a constructive and hopeful policy can take hold.

The major premise is the necessity of finding peaceful solutions, and avoiding the intolerable alternative of submission or a third World War. That is, unless we are willing to trust the survival of civilization to the chance that the great powers would carry on a war in which both sides have the weapons of atomic, chemical and bacteriological warfare, and neither uses them, for fear of retaliation or for other reasons. To appreciate how slim that chance is, one need only note that it means that one side goes to defeat, holding these weapons unused, despite the fact that the atom bomb, a least, gives the first user so great an advantage that it

3

might decide a conflict. We have, to be sure, the precedent of gas, which was not used in the last war; but that is not conclusive, since gas is a much less decisive weapon, offering correspondingly less temptation to a hard pressed combatant to use it.

A reasonably assured peace hinges on ultimate attainment of something for which the world is obviously not ready: namely, surrender of some part of the sovereign rights of independent states in a federal world government, much stronger than the United Nations is at present. It has to control the means of war, and the approaches to it (which means international inspection), while leaving complete national independence in other basic matters, so that the structure might include systems as far apart as the (future) Russian and the (future) American economies and national governments. However difficult this is, and however long it might take, it would be fatal to assume at the start that it is impossible. And it might be equally fatal, in view of Russia's suspicions, to press prematurely for the full ultimate program. In the immediate future, the logic of the atom bomb requires peace with Russia—friendly cooperation if possible, but in any case peace.

Prerequisite to substantial progress is willingness on each side, and confidence in the other's willingness. Obviously, this does not exist at present. At best, its development will take time, during which much needs to happen to build up the needed confidence and willingness; and much can happen to destroy the whole structure. We have a task of gaining time and using it; of saving the United Nations without—for the sake of saving its empty shell— abandoning all its main permanent functions of collective protection against aggression, and its temporary purposes of postwar economic reconstruction. We need to avoid the ultimate fatal disaster long enough, and to use the interval wisely enough to enable existing attitudes to change enough to permit success. Nations aspiring to freedom from totalitarian domination have a threefold task: to check a current Soviet drive for conquest, to put their own houses in order, and to work toward the development of the institutions and the altered attitudes which are necessary to world peace.

The prospect for changed attitudes is not bright, though to abandon it would be suicidal. Since 1935, major changes have taken place in the attitudes, both of the western powers and of Russia, as we shall see in a moment. If a major war can be staved off for another ten years, other changes might take place. But they start with Russia as our embittered adversary. Totalitarianism of the right has been conquered, only to leave us facing totalitarianism of the left.

2. NATURE OF THE TOTALITARIAN THREAT

Keeping in mind peace as the paramount objective, it is neither wise nor safe to underestimate the obstacles in its way, or to fail to understand them. It becomes vital to understand the nature of the threat which totalitarianism now offers; and this is a two-sided task. First, it is necessary to appreciate frankly the weaknesses of our own system, and to open our minds to see as clearly as possible the points which a sincere and clearheaded advocate of totalitarian principles might urge as superiorities of his alternative. This bears on the task of bringing our system, and those of nontotalitarian countries generally, to a condition of health and strength in which they will deserve to survive, and will be able to survive on the basis of a fair and frank comparison of advantages and disadvantages. Second, it is necessary to face the facts of life sufficiently to realize that the contest will not be waged on this ideal basis of fair and frank comparison: to appraise the actual forces opposing us and, so far as we can usefully conjecture, the motives behind them, and the expert and organized methods of conspiratorial aggression against which democracy has to defend itself.

The direct threat to this country is, in its more serious aspects, a deferred matter, as was Hitler's. The immediate threat is to Europe, plus Turkey and Iran, with a baffling problem in China and Korea and a dilemma full of dynamite in Palestine. Enveloping these is the threat to the United Nations, which was not set up to prevent or suppress aggression by any of the big five (permanent members of the Security Council, who have veto power) but will collapse if unchecked aggression by any of the big five takes place. That may sum up its most serious dilemma. And the United Nations is the present safeguard of the indispensable peace—together with the temporary war exhaustion of the great powers.

When I say "threat," I am not speaking of economic collectivism as a threat to private enterprise, but of totalitarianism as a threat to personal freedom and democracy. We in this country are properly defending, not private enterprise as it is—and it is not now fully "private"—but the right to develop and modify it by evolutionary methods, or at least by free and democratic methods, into something we hope will be more sound and satisfactory than the particular stage which quasi-private enterprise has now reached, or, for that matter, any of the stages that have preceded it. All democratic forces are our natural allies, including democratic socialists. Moscow has shown itself as much their enemy as ours.

This leads to one more premise, perhaps a statement of faith, not susceptible of proof. The world can exist with systems of economic collectivism and of (qualified) private enterprise. It can probably exist with democratic and autocratic systems, though autocracies contain serious inherent dangers to peace. It cannot exist with separate great sovereignties, some of which are bent on aggressive conquest.

3. HOW THE CRISIS CAME ABOUT: MARXIST ORIGINS

Of the two totalitarianisms we have faced, that of the right and that of the left, that of the left was first in the field. Marxian communism is only one form of collectivism, and the Soviet government developed from one wing only of Marxian-influenced thinking. Under Marx, communism was originally a revolt against mid-nineteenth-century industrialism, by the method and philosophy of class warfare as distinct from "utopian" socialism. It was led by intellectuals on behalf of the industrial "proletariat." This class was conceived, actually or potentially, as the majority, who need only organize to take over industry, after mass industry had come to dominate the economy. By an accident of history— or perhaps not by accident—it came to power, not in a country where industrialism was fully developed, but in one where the "capitalist" middle class was weak: in an almost feudal agricultural country, where the urban industrial proletariat was nearly non-existent, and had almost to be created.

Marx set the pattern of doctrinal orthodoxy by purging dissenters among his own small group. He also set a pattern of opportunist tactics, sending emissaries to Germany to organize Communist cells, which were to appear in the guise of liberal organizations. Both these qualities found characteristic expression in the Russian revolution of 1917. There the Bolsheviks, a minority wing of revolutionaries, trained in the harsh school of underground conspiracy, experienced in "uprising as an art," staged a coup d'état, disclaiming confiscatory aims and working solely with a "slogan of the day"—"peace and bread." They were supported by some twenty thousand war weary soldiers and sailors, to whom the slogan was an ideal appeal. They worked with the other radicals— social revolutionaries and Mensheviks—until the first election gave the Bolshevik faction a minority in the constituent assembly, on which they dissolved the assembly by force. From then on, they ruled.

4. AMERICAN REACTION TO THE BOLSHEVIK REVOLUTION

Our reaction was not friendly, and the memories of this undoubtedly add a third element to Russian suspicions of us, already rooted both in the Russian character and in the Marxian doctrine of irrepressible conflict. We supported anti-Bolshevik Russians, as part of the confused activities of the international expeditions to

Archangel and Siberia, in which we joined. Of this whole ill-informed, ill-conceived and ill-fated pair of adventures, perhaps the less said the better.[1] The best that can be said is that we were sincere in our professions of respect for Russia's sovereignty and territorial integrity (with reservations as to our Japanese partners in the Siberian venture) and our genuine purpose in Siberia was to protect the exit of the Czechoslovak troops (as to their need of protection, we may have been victims of interested misinformation). As to our official policy of non-intervention in Russian internal affairs, the record is inconsistent. At first, we were probably interested in supporting any group that would continue the war against Germany, which the Bolsheviks had ended with the peace of Brest-Litovsk—we were ready to use Russians or Czechoslovaks to help us fight Germans, if we could find some who were willing to be so used.

After we stopped fighting Germany, we still supported anti-Bolshevik Russian factions, thereby probably helping solidify the Russian people against these factions. When it became clear that continuation would leave us supporting unrepresentative factions against the bulk of the Russian people, we withdrew, apparently exerting pressure on Japan to join in withdrawal, and abandon any hope we may conjecture her to have had for a Japanese supported puppet state in eastern Siberia. To that extent we may have protected Russian territory for the benefit of the Soviet regime; but we cannot expect the Russians to draw fine distinctions between participants in that enterprise.

We were slow to recognize the Soviet regime, but we found that in commercial dealings, the Russians lived up to their agreements. And we gained a degree of uneasy confidence that they might have genuinely adopted the idea of revolution in one country, in place of the older dogma of world revolution. Then came fascism, and Mussolini's bid for empire in Ethiopia.

[1] See J. L. Strakhovsky, Intervention at Archangel; and Gen. Wm. S. Graves, America's Siberian Adventure, esp. pp. xi, 5–10, 26, 127, 152, 262, 301–3, 346–51.

5. FROM LITVINOV TO MOLOTOV

In this crisis, Litvinov, as Russian foreign minister, stood in the League of Nations as the chief exponent of strong sanctions against Italy. Whether this was due to Russian weakness rather than good will may now be an idle question. At that time, the western powers were not willing to take military measures, nor to restrict particular economic interests to the extent required to make economic sanctions effective. As a result, the first move in the Fascist campaign of aggression was successfully launched, in Ethiopia. The same failure of collective action permitted Fascism to win Spain; the western powers being about as suspicious of the Communist leanings of the republicans as of Franco's Fascism.

In the sequel, Stalin swung to hard-boiled nationalism, and waged war on Finland for strategic defensive positions, knowing that the League would not stop him. The more disastrous sequel came in 1939, when he made the pact with Hitler which enabled Hitler to start the second World War, secure (for as long as he wished it) against war on two fronts. Motives are, of course, conjectural; but Stalin must surely have wanted time to strengthen his military power, and must have known that he was setting the "capitalist" powers off on a war in which they might shatter one another's strength. Did he know a victorious Hitler would attack him in his own good time, or was this provoked only by Stalin's demanding too much in the Balkans and the near East?[1] Whatever the answer, Stalin seems, for some time, and perhaps up to the time of Hitler's attack on Russia in June, 1941, to have carried out the pact without evasion.

The war against Finland enlisted our sympathy for the underdog, and admiration for the Finns' superb fighting qualities; and the Hitler-Stalin pact did not help cordial relations with either party; but Hitler's war against Russia aroused genuine admiration for the courage and endurance displayed by the Russian people,

[1] Written before the publication of captured German documents bearing on this question.

genuine feeling of friendship for them, and eagerness to coöperate like allies in postwar reconstruction. We were ready to accept the fact of the Soviet political and economic system and do business with it, making whatever adjustments might be necessary to promote trade between the two kinds of systems. We were still opposed to any forcible expansion of the Soviet rule, but pictured Russia as continuing its prewar willingness to keep the Communist dictatorship within Russian bounds. Events had aroused some uneasiness on this score, but we were eager to be reassured—perhaps over eager.

In short, in 1945, the western powers had reached an attitude in which they could probably have coöperated with the Russia of ten years previous. But the opportunity had passed, by one of those grimly ironic comedies of errors in timing which history seems fond of playing. It is dubious whether any country can truly coöperate with the Russia of 1948, or could have coöperated with the Russia of 1945.

6. APPEASEMENT AND THE CONSEQUENCES

At Yalta, we formally acquiesced in Russia's Balkan sphere of influence, with a proviso for free popular governments which depended entirely on Russian good faith, since we had no power to enforce it. It has been completely violated. Russia wanted a zone of "friendly states," and has acted as if governed by the major premise that no state could be friendly to Russia if it had any option in the matter. The option has been removed, and "friendship" enforced, by communist police. The pattern is consistent, with variations to suit particular conditions.

Votes are sought, especially by promising the peasants land (this, in Russia, had been the prelude to forced collectivization; and the Russian economist, Varga, found that the distributions had reduced productivity).[1] But a voting majority is nonessential; a basis for cabinet representation is sufficient. Communists from

[1] See New York Times, January 25, 1948.

the victim country are trained in Russia, then re-exported and forced into the government, the army and the police, the crucial ministries being those controlling police, justice and propaganda. Once this leverage is gained, popular government is doomed.

The pressures used to gain nominal consent are various, including threat of strikes by communist dominated unions. "Plots against the state" are charged, the "plots" consisting of any genuine opposition, or any friendly communication with the western powers, which have a moral obligation for the maintenance of free governments. Either is treated as treason and punished as such; leaders who do not surrender or escape are imprisoned or executed.[1] This process is known as "liberation," the resulting government is set up by the "will of the people."[2] No act of aggression has taken place!

The Kaiser wanted eastward expansion to offset the British Empire. Being old-fashioned and deficient in ruthlessness by modern standards, his government and its legitimate successors could very likely not have held this territory permanently, in the face of the world trend which has ushered Britain out of India. The first World War saved eastern Europe from this fate, and reserved it to fall into the hands of a more absolute tyranny, with modern improvements, and one whose grip is likely to be more enduring. All of which illustrates poignantly how likely war is to make a bad thing worse, rather than cure it.

As to reconstruction of the rest of Europe, step after step toward common action has been blocked, until we awoke to the conviction that anything approaching effective coöperation was impossible as things stood; and our mood changed to one of shocked apprehension of what would happen to Europe as a result. The

---

[1] This list includes Mihailovitch (almost forgotten), Petkov (our protest at his death-sentence was "untactful"), Maniu, Nagy, Mikolajczyk and Jan Mazaryk. The story of Benes is unfinished as this is written. It is a complete catalogue of the genuinely domestic leaders of popular parties in the satellite countries.

[2] This fiction Henry Wallace is reported as accepting.

western powers are ready to surrender the supreme weapon—the atom bomb—and atomic power with it, to an international body, and to let their internal operations be subject to international inspection; and Russia is standing stiffly against this encroachment on old-fashioned absolute (and obsolete) sovereignty.

Any blame for Russia in all this may well be tempered by the memory of the responsibility of the western powers in the years following Mussolini's attack on Ethiopia. But that does not solve the present impasse. Everything has been done to convince us, against our earnest desires and hopes, that we face a second enemy bent on world conquest. If this is the case, we have already gone through the stage of Munich, at Yalta, Teheran and Potsdam. Little room is left for further retreat.

7. COMPARISON OF SYSTEMS: ALL CONTAIN INCONGRUITIES

Both kinds of totalitarianism are incongruous mixtures of opposites. So is private enterprise; so, probably, are most major social structures. Private enterprise is justified, in theory, by a humane goal of service to all, to be brought about through a mechanism originally conceived as one of free play for selfishness and the Devil take the hindmost, under Malthus' biological principle of poverty through overpopulation, which offered scanty prospects of improvement for the masses. This conflict of humane goal and selfish means is perhaps the major incongruity of private enterprise, underlying the various other "contradictions of capitalism," highlighted by Marxism in rebuttal to the "harmonies" discovered in it by defenders such as the French optimist Bastiat. Contradictions exist, harmony can never be either perfect or automatic; but reform and enlightenment have struggled toward reconciliation, and must go on struggling, under private enterprise or any other system.

The incongruities of Marxian communism are no less striking. It purports to be coldly "scientific" and realistic; and was based on a pre-scientific philosophy of history which has been erected into an unquestionable article of dogmatic faith, superior to factual evidence. Thus its "truths" about the world today, and especially about other countries, are still basically derived from a Bible eighty to one hundred years old. Its twin principles are orthodoxy and opportunism. Its philosophy was based on Hegel, with radical alterations, and ignored the concept of evolution, which was being made into a keystone of scientific thinking by Marx's contemporary, Darwin.

It was an anti-ethical philosophy of historical determinism, powered by a tremendous moral force, a theory that said: "Let history work its inevitable results," and became the most powerful weapon in a purposive campaign to see to it that the results should fulfil the prophecy. Its moral force was so dominated by indignation against wrong and injustice that there was little room for the humanity and good will that must underlie its millennial goal of a "classless state," whose coercive functions shall have "withered away." In this goal, its enemies would all have vanished, by liquidation or conversion; but it is lost without enemies to denounce and to blame for inevitable failures and shortcomings, so that when the enemies have been liquidated, it has to create fresh ones. It must include all humanity, but rules out all who deviate in the least from the pattern set by a select and self-constituted minority. Marx himself was moved by tremendous indignation on behalf of the dignity of the individual, which capitalism debased; and current sovietism, in his name, has effaced individual dignity more utterly than any other system. Its aspiration is democratic, in the sense of government for the people; and is embodied in the tightest and most ruthless despotism ever known, which can hardly be imagined as surrendering its power peaceably.

It set up the strongest internationalism in history, now placed at the service of Russian nationalism, the most aggressive extant, making a uniquely dangerous combination. It is utter materialism; and one of its advantages over us is in the moral realm. Yet its morality is the negation of morality as we understand it, for in it the end justifies any means. It is an unmoral morality and an anti-religious religion.

8. THE TWO BRANDS OF TOTALITARIANISM: OF THE RIGHT AND LEFT

The kinship of Nazism and Stalinism has become a commonplace—in countries where it can be safely mentioned. Elsewhere, the identity of American democracy with fascism or Nazism is equally commonplace. Nazism borrowed from sovietism and made improvements, some of which in turn have been adapted and improved on by the Soviets. But while similarities are inescapable, the thing to hunt for is differences: specifically, differences which may make it possible to do business with the Soviets, as it was not possible to do business with Hitler. They are not easy to find, but they do exist.

Each system represents an aggressive nationalism, with long frustrated ambitions to expand, and a feeling of "encirclement"; and each arms this nationalism with material command of the nation's total resources, backed by a revolutionary gospel and a conspiratorial technique. In Russia's case, a vast land area is uniquely lacking in unobstructed outlets to the sea, making a sense of geographical frustration and confinement understandable. Perhaps one of the chief differences is that with Nazism revolution was clearly incidental to conquest, and with Sovietism conquest may possibly take second place to world revolution. But this difference may not help much toward peace, so long as revolution and world conquest are viewed as inseparable, in whatever order of logical priority.

The Nazis had a master race and a master social-economic system, with the accent on race. The Soviets have a superior nationality, fairly inclusive racially, though with a pan-Slavic element and traces of anti-Semitism; and a master social-economic system, with the accent on the system and on its economic aspects. How does this differ from the attitudes of typical "Anglo-Saxons," who often have a feeling of racial or national superiority, and think their social and economic system better than others? The difference appears when a nation is dominated by a militant, messianic mission of expansion by forcible subjugation, backed by a coercive system for making this attitude unanimous and suppressing doubt and dissent.

America is not without traces of the messianic mission, visible in the attitude which proposes that we shall give no aid to Europe until the European nations have all made their systems over into copies of ours, or of what we should like ours to be. One saving fact is that we could not agree on the specifications to which Europe should be compelled to conform.[1] This attitude is a danger, but a negative one: an obstacle to positive international coöperation, not a threat of aggressive war. Its most serious aspect lies in giving support to Soviet claims that the "Marshall plan" is an American device to subjugate and enslave Europe. If we want to make that lie come partly true, that is an excellent way to go about it, and to insure the failure of the plan.

Nazism and Sovietism each set up a new ruling class, and new oppressed classes. Some of the labels are different. The Soviet rulers have a proletarian instead of a middle-class background; but for the present purpose the chief effect of this may be to add to the genuineness of their suspicion of all middle-class governments, which they designate indiscriminately as "fascist." In any case, after a social revolution has been in power for a generation, the former class origins will have lost much of their meaning. The ruling class will be recruited from the new classes of officials, technicians, intellectuals and manual workers; and mainly from what can fairly be called the new middle class.

Divergences of interest are not ended. Hitler, the fanatic, was

[1] One of the most extreme examples of this attitude is Henry Hazlitt's "Will Dollars Save the World?" Hazlitt's ultra-laissez-faire views are well known. Before enforcing them on Europe, his first difficulty would be to induce his own country to accept them.

surrounded by self-seeking opportunists and voluptuaries, and his unified state masked a welter of conflicting personal power-empires. This was perhaps the Achilles' heel of his system. In the Soviet state, these elements are less in evidence. The ruling group and the bureaucracy stay on their jobs, and there are no Hermann Goering steel works. The rulers have luxuries—not on Goering's scale, but when they are measured against the condition of the underprivileged masses, not to mention conditions in the Russian slave labor camps, they may constitute more substantial inequality than do our great incomes, shrunken as these are by the income tax. Where the few can command important comforts and conveniences, while the many lack what we should consider the bare necessities of tolerable existence, real inequality is greater than where the many have the basic necessities, and most of them a substantial margin over, and the few are differentiated by the command of less essential luxuries. Literal inequality of wages appears to be of comparable order of magnitude in Russia and this country, inequality in Russia being greater in some trades and less in others. Between 1928 and 1934 it increased slightly.[1] In the Russian army, inequality between officers and privates is much greater than in ours.

This inequality is apparently not a mere temporary concession to opportunistic necessity. The Soviets have adopted the idea of differential incentives as an essential feature of their economy, characteristically stigmatizing the former "levelling tendencies," once they had given them up, as "survivals of capitalistic thinking," though they stem from the authority of Marx himself.[2] The natural

[1] See Abram Bergson, "Distribution of the Earnings Bill Among Industrial Workers in the Soviet Union," Journal of Political Economy, April, 1942, pp. 227–250.

[2] See K. Ostrovitianov, "Basic Laws of Development of Soviet Economy," in Science and Society, IX (1945) pp. 238–42, 249. Cf. Oscar Lange, "The Working Principles of the Soviet Economy, Russian Economic Institute, 1944, cited by J. J. Spengler, in "The Role of the State," Jour. of Econ. History, Supplement VII, 1947, p. 125. In a new journal, edited by Ostrovitianov, G. Koslov has apparently taken the step of explicitly "revising" Marx and Engels, in favor of the views of Lenin and Stalin, on this matter of differential pay. (New York Times, June 20, 1948).

inference is that it is not the exploitation of the masses that is objected to, but exploitation by the wrong people, under the wrong system: by private enterprise, with its (dwindling) layer of "leisure-class" supernumeraries, instead of by a "proletarian" bureaucracy with its overhead of technicians, favored and subservient intellectuals, army and police.

In both systems, self-interest persists, and continues to interfere with collective efficiency, mostly at different points and in different ways. The Nazi system was honeycombed with corruption; in the Soviets, personal self-interest is divided between gaining advancement and avoiding the dangers that go with it: staying out of the bad graces of the secret police, and cultivating the bureaucratic art of protecting one's record. This in turn is divided between production records and political ones. Gauging the picture as best one can, it seems that an American is warranted in feeling that under our system, with all its defects, self-interest is on the whole enlisted in channels more positively and constructively relevant to efficient productive performance.

Nazism had numerous sources of strength, among which we may enumerate four potent weapons against its enemies, resting on two basic characteristics of its system; and three strong appeals to its own people. All these Russia shares, and some it has improved on. First, as to the weapons; they include mechanized blitzkrieg, the fifth column, action by unofficial and unacknowledged agencies, and utter ruthlessness and bad faith. They rest on the power of total control of the nation's resources, and the secrecy made possible by this and by dictatorship.

Mechanized warfare had long been technically possible, but the cost of utilizing it fully appeared prohibitive to any democratic country, depending on customary methods of finance, and unwilling to lay on the people a fiscal load of unheard-of magnitude. The Nazi economic and fiscal system, despite falling far short of total mobilization (partly because of the leaders' personal profiteering) was able to do what had been thought impossible, and produced blitzkrieg, irresistible to any power not prepared in kind. Forced to imitate or succumb, the British restricted civilian consumption more strictly than the Nazis, and utilized women in war work more fully.[1] The Russian economy also employs total mobilization. It has a smaller available margin above bare necessities, but is readier to enforce harsh restrictions on the masses, in the interest of its army and its foreign agencies, which are amply supplied. In fact, there can be little doubt that the working masses have a larger percentage of "surplus value" subtracted from their product than "capitalism" subtracts. The added weapon of surprise attack, which staggered us at Pearl Harbor, has now become even more formidable.

The Nazi use of the fifth column needs no comment. The Soviets have improved the technique. Instead of merely opening the gates to an invading military, their fifth columns are often capable of carrying out a conquest without overt aid. They are a rigorously trained and disciplined, but unofficial, army, with an expertness and an indefatigable energy in conspiratorial methods of minority rule, exploiting the vulnerable features of free and democratic coöperation and sabotaging its indispensable fundamentals. In subduing the satellite countries, the fifth columns have done the bulk of the work.

Totalitarianism virtually wipes out the distinction between official and unofficial agencies, permitting the government to conceal and evade responsibility for its acts, whenever that may seem expedient. At home, the party and the press are only the most outstanding and tangible examples of agencies virtually but not formally part of the government. In foreign relations, the Comintern and its successor, the "Cominform," have served this purpose, while the activities and personnel which they have coördinated are omnipresent and nameless.

This elusiveness is complemented by the weapons of ruthlessness and bad faith. By them there is much profit to be gained

[1] This refers to the period before Speer became economic dictator in Germany.

in international dealings, up to a point and at a price. The price includes solidifying the opposition of all who are still free to oppose totalitarian conquest, plus rapid progress toward a complete breakdown of international dealings, as contracts lose their value. Hitler reached this point; the Soviets have not yet quite done so, though they have made dangerous progress in that direction. As a minor incident, they have surpassed the Nazis in another respect, setting a new high in international bad manners.

To the people, in addition to employment, Nazism offered two things: promise of a resurrection of the German nation and, for the individual, a sense of playing an integral part in a great national enterprise. These have their counterparts, in altered form, in the soviet system. And we had best face the fact that this fills a need for the individual, which the individualistic philosophy and private enterprise do not fill. This appeal does not reach all individuals; but those whom it does reach are given a sense of purpose: absorbed into an objective bigger than themselves. The Nazi purpose was Satanic; the Soviets offer an ultimate goal of universal salvation, to be somehow reached by means that include the systematic wiping out of both truth and humanity. If such a goal is achieved by such means, it will probably be for the first time in human history. This absorption in a common purpose gives substance to what the Soviets mean by "democracy," and it is not wise for us to despise it or judge it a total sham, merely because it reverses our meaning of the term. Perverted as it is, it gives their system a strength which points to the greatest weakness in our own system: a weakness that must be repaired if our system is to be sound and strong.

9. THEORIES OF INDIVIDUAL AND STATE: A FALSE ANTITHESIS

The contrast of systems has been dramatized by opposing the theory that the individual is nothing and the community and the state everything, and the theory that the community is nothing but the arithmetic sum of the individuals who compose

it, and the state their agent. This is a false antithesis.[1] Even the
Nazis have claimed that they were fundamentally concerned with
the development of the individual, and were merely wiser than the
avowed individualists as to how to promote this end. They realized
that the individual can reach his fullest development only as a
part of a social whole. And this is, in principle, true. Incidentally,
the Nazi system gave a larger place to the interests of posterity
than individualism does in practice. This also is sound, though the
character of their ambition for posterity was not. The question is
how the community ends shall be determined.

The real contrast is not between these false absolutes, nor even
between leadership and mass rule. It puts on one side systems in
which community purposes are set by leadership responsible and
responsive to the wills of the people, by a process in which rival
ideas and purposes compete in a field not too restricted or too
unfair. This is the key to a democratic system as we undestand it.
A system which trusts the people to this extent will naturally lean
toward trusting them as far as practicable to look after their individual economic interests, though the scope of this may change
with changing industrial conditions. So democracy and private
enterprise have a kinship, but are not identical.

On the other side stands the system in which community purposes are determined by dictatorship, and discussion is forcibly
limited to conformity with these purposes, thus preventing them
from being responsible or responsive to popular will. Careers may
be open to talent—another test of democracy—but they are
careers in serving these dictator-given purposes, by dictator-given
methods.

10. REVOLUTIONARY MORALITY, AND THE "BIG LIE"

The Nazis borrowed from Marxian communism the code by
which the revolutionary end justifies all means and is the one
supreme test of morality. This means complete unmorality toward

[1] I have discussed this briefly in Alternative to Serfdom, pp. 20-21.

all but the comrades in the revolutionary enterprise: things are good if the ruling race, or the right party, does them; and the same things are bad if others do them, in which case they are called by different names. In practice it has meant hierarchical gradations of unmorality toward various levels among its supporters, down to the masses who are pawns of its power politics. It was obvious that those who constructed the Nazi myths and propaganda could not have believed them in quite the same sense as the rank and file were enjoined to do—even allowing for one's capacity to be hypnotized by one's own propaganda.[1] Communist ideology has had generations in which to strike down the kind of roots that go deeper than reason; accordingly, even to those who engineer the occasional puzzling lightning changes of the communist party line, we may concede a high percentage of sincere belief in the messianic mission which these changes are aimed to serve. That, in fact, is precisely what makes this unmoral morality so much more formidable than mere unscrupulousness could be.

Almost worse than material ruthlessness has been the wholesale murder of truth, through systematic adoption of the theory and practice of the "big lie" as an instrument of policy, supreme and permeating all life, with suppression of all but the officially-sanctioned lie, which centered on a propaganda of hate, contempt and calumny toward all free and democratic peoples. "Truth is a bourgeois prejudice." The official lie has been built into a supreme and unquestionable credo, backed by all the resources of science, applied science, pseudo-science and (in the Nazi case at least) mythology.

The meaning of words is destroyed by perversion and inversion, but this soon loses its effect. One simply learns, for example, that in the Nazi language "warmonger" is the term for anyone who expresses any objection to Nazi conquest. The Soviets have widened the assault. Dictatorship (if of proletarian origin) becomes

---

[1] Goebbels' diary confirms this. See review by H. R. Trevor-Roper, New York Times, March 14 1948, Magazine Section, pp. 9, 57.

"democracy" and democracy, "fascism." Soviet conquest, by the methods which have become stereotyped in the satellite countries, is a "domestic matter," the process of liquidating opposition leaders and clamping the lid of terror on their followers is "liberation," aid to a victim, if ineffective, is "interfering in other nations' internal affairs," if effective, it becomes "imperialist aggression." Normal democratic opposition is "plotting against the state" and becomes particularly heinous if aggravated by any friendly communication with other powers which have joined with the Soviets in agreements for the preservation of freedom and democracy. An attempt to keep areas of the world open for normal commercial and personal intercourse is a "plot for fascist world conquest"; and so on, ad nauseam.

These methods have had their drawbacks for the users. The monopoly of lying has a deteriorating effect on the quality of discourse, leading to a habit of substituting epithet for evidence and vehemence for verification. The result is not notably effective in swaying free minds which have alternative versions to select from, or wills that are still free to choose their course of action. But while few outside the orbit of Soviet supremacy may be deceived by these perversions, one does not have to be deceived to see that some of them contain a shred of substance. The part of wisdom for us—and a hard part it is—is to look searchingly for that shred of truth, and eliminate whatever affords a basis for it. We should refuse to dismiss the matter with the easy belief that these distortions are exclusively beamed at the Russian home consumer. That may be the largest market, but a more important one consists of persons in countries still free, who are suspicious of us and disposed toward believing colorable accusations. It behooves us to keep our record very clear.

The tactic of accusing your opponent of what you intend doing to him, and getting your accusation in first, ingenious though it is, has been overworked, until its chief effect is in disclosing Soviet intentions, and its chief defect the fact that the indication is not invariably dependable. Otherwise, Soviet accusations that we are planning aggressive war on them would be more disturbing than they are, as indications of their designs. The bright side of this is its indication that the Soviets must actually have vast confidence in our peaceful intentions; otherwise they would not provoke us so grossly and wantonly. Such indications would be more enlightening if we could tell when an accusation is conscious fiction and when the Russian sincerely believes it of us, because it is what he would do in our place. As a minor instance, when a Russian refuses to believe that the masses of autos outside an American factory belong to the workers (because, according to current Marxism, "capitalism" could not enrich the workers to that extent) and thinks they are a staged exhibit, it is at least suggestive that his own government may have used the technique of staged exhibit on occasion.

One enlightening episode culminated while these lectures were being delivered. On January 25, 1948, the New York Times announced the disgrace of the eminent Russian economist, Eugene Varga, and the abolition of the institute he had headed, as a result of the erroneous findings of a survey he had made of wartime and postwar world economy. With him were disgraced twenty other prominent economists who had participated in a conference to discuss these findings because, while none of them had fully agreed with Varga, they had not condemned his findings completely, as they should have done. They were deficient in the duty of "Soviet self-criticism."[1]

The findings? Firstly, that in the long run, capitalism is doomed to follow the laws of Marxian development. But for conditions during the war, and for a prognosis for the first postwar decade, Varga made the mistake of following the evidence of facts. Among his findings were the following. While there will be postwar recessions, there is no likelihood that the basic crisis of capitalism will

[1] This casts an interesting light on the claim, often made, that "Soviet self-criticism" affords some latitude for deviant ideas. Here it implies the precise opposite: a duty to suppress deviation.

appear until after 1955. The war showed that democratic capitalist states, in emergency and under favorable political conditions, can practice effective control in the interest of the whole economy, subordinating monopolistic interests. The position of their more "exploited" workers improved substantially. Much colonial exploitation was abolished or mitigated. The British Labor party has achieved postwar legislation opposed to the interests of the capitalist class. The "agrarian reforms" in eastern Europe did not fundamentally change the structure of the agricultural economies, but reduced agricultural productivity, and it will take ten years to regain prewar levels.

Not startling, perhaps; but in Russia these are economic errors by party ruling. They not only violate the accredited Marxian orthodoxy; they grossly contradict the reports of current conditions daily disseminated by the Soviet propaganda machine. Next day's "Times" announced a campaign against "obsequiousness toward western bourgeois culture," while Pravda criticized Varga's views as "tantamount to denying the action of spontaneous economic laws on the development of capitalism," opening the way to holding that the bourgeois state could overcome these laws, and overcome depressions and unemployment. This was treated as self-evident error. Next day, in the United Nations Subcommission on Freedom of the Press, the Russian representative first urged that publication of fascist ideas be forbidden (note common Soviet use of "fascism" and "capitalism" as coextensive terms) and later urged this country to study communism more objectively—indicating that he meant free of unfavorable judgments—ending with the claim: "We study capitalism objectively." It is to be presumed that he said this with a straight face, though knowing that he was speaking to people who had had every opportunity to read the news of the Varga episode.

Ten days later (New York Times, February 8) appeared a notice that Varga is now editing "World Economy and World Politics," and expressing therein strongly anti-capitalist ideas, presumed to be satisfactory to the Kremlin. This incident appears, on the whole, hopeful. First, there are people in Soviet Russia who care enough for factual evidence to run some risks on its account. Second, Varga's findings have circulated among Russian high officials, and some of them must know, though not for publication, that they are true to fact and objective as to the ten-year forecast. Some such recognition would seem to be reflected in the lenient treatment of Varga's heresy.

11. DIFFERENCES OF DEGREE ARE IMPORTANT

In making a frank comparison of both Nazism and sovietism with our own system we shall, if we can be objective enough, find first that both totalitarianisms have a substratum of care for the interests of the masses, as the rulers see those interests. Secondly, many of the differences are matters of degree: it is not all black and white. But, thirdly, these differences of degree are vitally important; and many differences are more than matters of degree, they are matters of the direction in which the main conscious drive aims. It follows, fourthly, that we must defend things that are imperfect, but capable of improvement, against things that are immeasurably worse, and tending in what we consider a wrong direction.

One of the worst things we can do is to lean over backward so far in the pursuit of objectivity that we can see no differences—nothing seems very different from anything else. The Communist "party line" at present is skillfully playing on this vulnerable joint in the democratic armor: trying, for example, to convince us that the Russian subjugation of its zone of satellite countries is no different from our own attempts to induce friendship and support for us in the Latin-American countries.

If we really imitated Russia in this area, the difference between this and our present policy would be glaringly apparent. It is true that our expressed wishes sometimes have more coercive force than we ourselves are aware; and one of the things we have to do is to keep this in mind, and school ourselves to exercise corresponding restraint. But if we seriously overstep these bounds, the attitudes of our neighbor countries will soon make us aware of it—as Panama recently demonstrated, in refusing us aviation bases outside the Canal Zone. Their cooperation rests on their confidence in our restraint. If we ever really imitate the methods used to subdue the Russian satellite zone, complete from American trained fifth columns to fabricated "plots" and liquidations of political opponents, it may be time to speak about seeing no difference between our policy and the one eastern Europe is facing. There are differences. They involve the issue of truth and falsehood, right and wrong, humanity and inhumanity, freedom—admittedly imperfect—and servitude.

CHAPTER II

INTERPRETING THE THREAT
AND MEETING IT

1. "THE POLICE STATE IS RUSSIAN, NOT COMMUNIST"

The police state is sometimes palliated on the ground that Russia cannot be governed in any other way, or that the Russians do not know how to govern in any other way. It is sometimes added that the Bolsheviks did not invent the secret police; the Czars used it, and when their government broke up, some equivalent was needed. The implication is that the Russians have a police state because they are Russian and ex-czarist, not because they are communist. There may be a good deal in these contentions, though it is not clear how they make the prospect of the forcible spread of the Soviet system any more pleasant for the potential or actual victims.

The idea that Russians can be governed in no other way belies the great capacities of the Russian people, and their considerable development of institutions of local self-government. The same idea, applied to the satellite countries, probably libels the people there, who produced the leaders who are now dead or in exile. It would certainly be a libel on Czechoslovakia, Finland and all countries west of them, including Germany. And it is not fair to judge the Russian people by the behavior of those who reach the highest positions of power under a Marxian "ideology." To do that would be to ignore the fact that a system of government brings to power those whose natural qualities suit its requirements and characteristics, or who can and do conform, whatever their natural leanings might be.

The Russians are not all Molotovs or Vishinskys: their system brings such persons to the top. And if we had a fascist or a soviet system here, it could and would find plenty of willing instruments of police repression, either people who enjoy brutality or who are willing followers of a ruthless "ideology." Most of us are not like that; but most of us would not be trusted with responsible positions under such a system. Humane persons might be shocked at what could happen in our own existing police forces, if the authorities merely began to encourage "third degree" methods instead of restraining them.

The real question about any system is, which way is it facing, and in what direction is it moving? If police-state methods are now required, is Stalinism working toward a condition in which they can be relaxed or dispensed with? Theoretically, yes—in a future state in which all shall have taken the true doctrine as the rule of their lives. Practically, the standards of orthodoxy are so rigid and detailed that no mere inner acceptance could possibly generate the degree of uniformity that is insisted on. Practically, the police state has been intensified in Russia beyond the dreams of the czars, and has been applied to other countries which are unquestionably able to rule themselves without it, if it is merely a matter of maintaining order and giving the people the kind of government that suits them.

That brings us to another justification for the police state, derived not from Russian history and character, but from the requirements of a collectivist revolution. The idea is that such a drastic and far-reaching economic change, to be successful, needs to be pushed through at the highest possible speed which coercively unified effort permits; and even so it will take a considerable time, during which it needs stable tenure, so that it may survive the pains of transformation, until the deferred benefits of successive five-year plans have a chance to appear. In short, the police state is the price of revolutionary speed of change. There may be something in that; but it is hard to separate it from the fact that the kind and degree of change that has taken place was one that only a small minority actively wanted, and from the further fact that benefits for the masses have been indefinitely deferred by devoting much of the heavy industry to war material.

A country that has the patience to move gradually does not need the police state; and there are many advantages about moving gradually and feeling one's way. Even such an ostensible reform as breaking up great estates and distributing the land to peasants has its pitfalls if carried out abruptly, without clear foresight of the reactions it involves. The country, including peasants, cannot eat more unless more grain is produced; and peasants will not voluntarily part with grain unless the other industries are producing, and making available to the peasants, goods they are willing to take in exchange for their grain. If they find the money that is offered them will buy nothing, they keep their grain (if they can), and the cities go hungry. If the government seizes grain by the methods used in the thirties, in the most acute period of its struggle with the peasants, millions of peasants die of hunger. The collectivization of Russian agriculture was forced at a pace that far outstripped the peasants' willing consent, and Russia paid a terrible price. It would seem inherently impossible to prove whether this price has bought more progress in productivity than could have been secured in the same thirty years by more gradual and voluntary methods. In the acute stages of the struggle, productivity suffered heavily.

In England, on the other hand, the Fabians had the patience of gradualism; and the generation following is witnessing far-reaching results, without the police state. It is understandable how a convinced collectivist would be unwilling to wait that long. But I believe the American verdict, like the British, would be that, if greater speed requires the police state, the price is too heavy.

2. WHAT TO BELIEVE AS TO THE SOVIETS' INTENTIONS

What do the Soviets portend for the rest of the world? With Soviet Russia as with Nazi Germany, there is the same dilemma as to what to believe. Shall we believe the revelations, in printed page and in action, of purpose of world conquest for a communist system ruled from Moscow, and of firm belief that the same world cannot contain capitalist and communist countries?[1] Shall we believe the revelations of what revolutionary morality means? Or shall we trust the occasional conciliatory professions that Russia wants peace (Hitler also wanted peace), that there is no occasion for war, and that the countries of the world can work together in the United Nations (complete with veto)?[2] Shall we believe in words or in actions, which often point in a different direction? The example of Hitler is not reassuring as a guide to an answer.

Twice we have been offered the choice—once by Litvinov and once by Hitler—between believing a printed dogma of ruthless war, or current diplomatic offers of a peaceful character. We appear to have chosen wrong both times, refusing to believe "Mein Kampf," but believing its Soviet equivalent and so refusing Litvinov's olive branch. It is particularly important not to guess wrong a third time.

If one assumes that the Soviets want a world-wide extension of their system, is there a limit beyond which the government would cease to be willing to pay the price in exposure of their personnel to alien influences? Or can they obviate this by using foreign agents trained in Moscow? Or if one assumes they merely want a safety zone of satellites, how soon would these become so identified with Russian interests as to require a further safety zone to protect them?[3] There is said to be a considerable migration of nonuni-

[1] For example, Stalin's "Problems of Leninism."

[2] For example, Stalin's interview with Stassen, or with eight British labor members of Parliament (New York Times, Oct. 18, 1947).

[3] As this is being revised, the papers carry news of the conversion of Czechoslovakia into a communist police state, with speculations as to whether the next victim will be Finland, Italy or France.

formed Russians to these countries. Is there any stopping place short of the ocean? Will it stop there?

At least, Russia has stayed in the United Nations, though the appointment of the prosecutor, Vishinsky, as Soviet delegate is about as reassuring as if we should appoint Col. McCormick as our ambassador to Great Britain. American officials, after long frustrating experience, have been driven to the extraordinary step of publicly charging—what had long been obvious—that Russia's role in the United Nations was to paralyze it for its proper functions, especially, at present, the promoting of European recovery. In the case of Germany, it has been particularly easy to utilize the postwar fears and resentments of the western countries to support a status loaded with obstacles to recovery which are calculated to kill hope and to lead to the kind of chaos which is a favorable prelude to Soviet absorption. Russia's price for permitting the unification of Germany—ten billions in current reparations plus a joint control in the Ruhr—was prohibitive on this ground.[1]

Russia may be expected to stay in the United Nations, if only because it is an unrivalled sounding board for propagandist speeches. And the other nations will presumably want Russia to stay in. This means several things. It means that the United Nations' agencies and activities which can really accomplish something will be limited to those which raise no serious conflict with Russia. We should make the most of these activities. Where conflict arises, the other countries will be forced either to accept frustration or to take important actions outside the United Nations framework: for instance, the "Marshall plan." This is unfortunate; it should be done only when a vital object cannot be gained in any other way, and even when it is necessary, every effort should be made to avoid discrediting the United Nations. Finally, the situation means that efforts to strengthen the United Nations—by limiting the veto or otherwise—will be limited, because if they go too far or too fast they will merely increase Russian suspicion and

[1] New York Times, Dec. 9, 1947.

hostility, which is the decisive factor limiting what can be accomplished. So they would do more harm than good.

3. THEORIES OF INEVITABLE WAR

The simpler theories of inevitable war are false; but that fact does not dispose of the danger that war might come; it merely means that, if it comes, it is likely to come in a more roundabout fashion than the simple theories represent. The majority of thinking people in Russia presumably believe that "capitalist" countries are forced to wars of aggression to palliate the weaknesses of their economic system, because that is Marxian dogma. In the nineteenth century, there was much to support it; today it is palpably false. Colonial empires are in retreat. Prevailing opinion here is not only overwhelmingly against such aggression, but forewarned against economic moves that might lead unintentionally in that direction. In recent years, we have allowed American investors' interests to suffer, rather than impair a "good neighbor" policy.

Democracies are not only not aggressive; they are almost fatally slow to take arms in defense, waiting until the aggressor has gained positions that put his intended victims at serious disadvantage. Those in charge of Soviet foreign policy are well aware of this, and will make the utmost use of it, meanwhile disseminating the opposite doctrine to their followers. Can time and the evidence of facts, slowly filtering through Russian censorship, ever disprove this doctrine, to minds with a vested interest in a will to believe otherwise? Can they do it before it is too late?

We are ready to stand on the results of a peaceful comparison of the merits of the two systems, including what we hope to be able to make of ours by nontotalitarian methods. Soviet Russia, by the test of her methods of expansion, is not. There are indications to support the theory that the shoe is on the other foot; that Russia is impelled to aggression to divert attention from some of the less attractive features of her system and from unrevealed discontents at home, to induce enduring of domestic privations and to furnish a scapegoat, perhaps to exterminate rival systems which stand up too well in the test of peaceful comparison.

It is true that Russia does not want a "shooting war." She is not ready for it; though if that were the only safeguard, ten or fifteen years would be a maximum estimate of the time we could count on. Meanwhile, however, they are proceeding to make their conquests by other methods, through the unofficial and unavowed agencies in the use of which they are so expert. It seems obvious that the Soviet hope is to proceed, by engineered coups d'état, to establish positions from which it would take armed invasion to dislodge them. Either they count on the nontotalitarian powers to stop short of that step, or they are ready to take the consequences. If a shooting war is inevitable, it will be because the Soviets are right as to what their present methods can accomplish, but wrong if they assume that there is no limit to the supineness of the western powers. Hitler finally miscalculated this limit—as any persistent aggressor seems bound to do, in the end. The chance of avoiding a shooting war depends on finding other ways in which the Soviet drive for conquest can be checked. This may be a platitude, but it defines the "calculated risk" on which the life or death of a free system depends.

4. CHARTING OUR COURSE: APPEASEMENT WILL NOT WORK

To start with, we should by now be able to identify strategies that will not work. One such is the policy of "appeasement," defined as surrendering to an aggressor what he wants to absorb today, in the hope that his appetite will be satisfied, and he will not demand more tomorrow. It is the policy in which the material gains always go to the same side, the other getting only promises and hopes. Whatever excuses may be made for past instances of this policy, by now experience has amply demonstrated that the hope is vain. If backed by a promise, the promise is proved worthless; belief in it is fatuous. And if one still had a will to believe in it, which overcame one's better judgment, which of the still free nations of Europe should we throw out of the sleigh?

Many critics of American policy are today urging that we should "reach an understanding with Russia"; the implication being that failure to come to mutually acceptable arrangements is wholly due to our unnecessarily hostile attitude. It is notable that this phrase is used by those who have not been facing the heartbreaking task of reaching agreements in actual negotiations, and giving effect to them afterward. A long list of obstacles could be drawn up, long and unprofitably discouraging. One of the toughest is a situation in which a failure of negotiations works for Russia's interests, as the Soviet government appears to conceive them. It blocks the world's recovery.

The implied objective of the "understanding" policy would seem to be to induce Russia, somehow, to name now her final price, coupled with the hope that it would be one we could accept, and the further hope that Russia would abide by it. For neither of these hopes does past experience afford the slightest basis. Another possible variant is the idea that Russian expansion is genuinely defensive in purpose, moved solely by fear of aggressive action by the "capitalist" powers; and if the Soviet government could be convinced, by someone in whom they had confidence, that the "capitalist" powers are really friendly, it would at least be satisfied with what it has already got, and settle down to doing business peaceably with the remaining "capitalist" countries. In all this, there is only one thing that appears credible: namely, that Russia has tried to induce several politically influential Americans to believe it.[1]

[1] It has been flatly asserted (U. S. News, Mar. 5, 1948, p. 13) in face of official disclaimers, that a Russian overture for a conference, looking to compose the "cold war," was made late in January and rejected. If such an offer was made, it should probably have been accepted, even though the only conceivable purpose of the offer was to confront us with another Munich, with Czechoslovakia once more as the victim. The steam roller which flattened Prague in three days in February, and completed its basic reorganization in

The only rational conclusion is that appeasement means submission to further absorptions, by thinly disguised force, of one democratic country after another, and that the only "understanding" that could be reached in the winter of 1947–8 would be one that would lead to that result. If the alternative is war, the choice is between two intolerables. Discounting the atom bomb, and thinking only of war's freshly proven capacity to make bad things worse instead of better, there is much to be said for a decision to submit, and let world unity come by the route of Soviet conquest. Recognizing that this would almost inevitably mean wiping out centuries of progress toward humanitarianism, freedom and democracy, and starting over again to rebuild what had been lost, there is still a considerable probability that this would be less of a setback to civilization than one more World War.

There seem to be two decisive reasons against adopting this policy. One is that it would probably not lead to peace, after all, because the democratic peoples are not all Gandhis. At some point, their resolve for nonresistance would crack, and war would come— probably after fatal concessions had already been made. The other reason is that there appears to be still a modest chance of avoiding both submission and war, though not by the path of appeasement. On what does that chance depend?

5. BASIC REQUIREMENTS FOR A TOLERABLE OUTCOME

At present, it appears that nothing will contain the Russian drive, short of an alliance for "collective self-defense," in the spirit of Article Fifty-One of the United Nations Charter, but without waiting, as this article might be taken to imply, for a literal armed attack to materialize, before forming the alliance. In addition,

---

twelve days more, was not improvised. It had been in preparation for years, long before there was a "Marshall plan." It was poised and ready at the time of the alleged offer of a conference. It is unthinkable that any inducement we could offer would have persuaded Stalin to spare Czechoslovakia, and even more unthinkable that our hypothetical refusal of this hypothetical offer was in any way responsible for his decision to move in, though his agents did seize a favorable occasion.

with the alliance to back them, the individual countries would be obliged to resist the first entering wedges of Soviet penetration, recognizing that once communists are in control of the ministries of police, education and propaganda, the battle is already lost. In short, it becomes the duty of the single country to resist all penetration short of armed invasion, trusting that an alliance would deter the aggressor from that step. This, and economic aid, seem to constitute the twin requirements for containing the Russian offensive.

This gains only a breathing space. The ultimate goal is an understanding; but that can come only if Russia really abandons plans of aggressive conquest, and to induce her to do that will take time. So the outcome depends on whether, in the breathing-space gained by containing the present drive, we can convince the Russian leaders (also reaching and convincing the people, if possible) by actions, not arguments, that the following things are true.

(1) That the free countries are too sound and strong to collapse or be captured. This could not be expected earlier than, let us say, 1955, when European reconstruction may be stabilized, and when the United States shall have passed through the acid test afforded by the substantial end of the first period of postwar rebuilding, and the resulting recession of industrial activity.

(2) That our system is willing and able to live and let live with that of the Soviets. This depends on policies that can come into being only with the containing of the present Russian drive.

(3) That therefore, to live and let live is the best Russian policy; that friendship is better than subjugation, and that actions should be made consistent with occasional professions to that effect. They might rediscover, after over thirty years, how strong an appeal there is in an offer of "peace and bread," which the people must surely crave as strongly as in 1917, as against a fomented fear of war,

and privations intensified by the maintaining of a huge war machine. Peace and bread would not now have to be bought, as in 1917, by territorial concessions.

In contrast, no good purpose seems to be served by publicly expressed hopes that the Soviet system contains the seeds of its own degeneration and breakdown, for which we may hopefully wait. Such expressions would of course serve to aggravate hostility. And the condition they anticipate, unless it came extraordinarily quickly, could be even more dangerous to the world than a condition of economic health.

One thing seems to give us a chance for the live-and-let-live outcome. Whereas Nazi Germany was ruled by a fanatic, a paranoiac, a mad genius, Soviet Russia appears to be ruled by men who, underneath their revolutionary credo, are coolly calculating opportunists, whose doctrinaire orthodoxy will not extend to butting their heads against a stone wall, once they recognize it as such. The "party line" has shown the capacity to change drastically overnight; and the Marxian scriptures are many-sided enough to afford a tolerable basis for any change of front that the leaders may decide is required by the realities of the situation.

On our side, this means readiness to make or permit adjustments of an economic sort in which Russia has an interest, so long as they do not wreck or overburden other economies, or carry the entering wedges of political and military absorption. This principle seems to govern our official policy, and should be lived up to in good faith. It applies to eastern oil, and to other matters, some of which may be even more difficult to compose.

We have a further duty to restrain gratuitously provocative utterances, especially any that might lend color to Russian charges that we are planning armed aggression. So far as I am aware, no one speaking for our government has furnished the slightest basis for these charges; but there have been examples of well-nigh incredible irresponsibility in unofficial utterance, some of them in high places.[1] We shall, of course, install no censorship, but the duty of voluntary restraint has been recognized by a United Nations resolution, unanimously passed on November 3, 1947, condemning war inciting propaganda. And on November 6, at the thirtieth anniversary of the Bolshevik revolution, both Molotov and Bulganin made speeches publicly accusing us of planning armed aggression.[2] Comment appears unnecessary.

As for the vital question of the atom bomb, any settlement of that must apparently wait for some alteration of attitudes, however urgent it is that the bomb be placed in safer hands than those of any national government. Russia's attitude is that of a man who says to his neighbor: "You ask that we turn over our guns to the judge and let him search us for concealed weapons. The only proper basis for peace is such mutual confidence that we could rely on one another's promises. (I know you are planning to shoot me, despite your assurances to the contrary.) So I demand that we simply agree to throw away our guns, and I do not consent to be searched. That must be left for later discussion. But first you must teach me to make that gun you have, which is more deadly than mine."

There is more than one possible interpretation of Russia's refusal of international control of atom splitting, some more disquieting than others. She is presumably aware that a mutual promise to disarm, uninspected and unenforced, would give a great advantage of secrecy to totalitarian countries, as against the accessibility of democratic systems. And she may not have the kind of imagination required to appreciate the brand of fear in-

[1] An outstanding example is an article by Representative Charles A. Eaton, Chairman of the House Foreign Affairs Committee, in the American Magazine for August, 1947. The ultimate in rocking the boat consists of utterances advocating a preventive war now, while we have the power. Mr. Jouett Shouse "almost" advocated this (N. Y. Times, Oct. 15, 1947). This would have to mean attack by atom-bombs, since we have no other superior military force. One wonders what targets the advocates of such a war would select, and how they would expect the attack to be followed up. One also wonders if they remember Archangel.

[2] N. Y. Times, Nov. 7, 1947.

spired in western countries by the thought of atom bombs in the hands of a country addicted to revolutionary morality, and to see that it is not to her interest to arouse that kind of fear. It would not bring about submission, but might provoke unpredictable and unsafe reactions, as it has already provoked an irresponsible few to advocate "preventive war."

A country really intending to live and let live might come to see, before it is too late, that to relieve the world of this fear is worth more to it than the advantage of superior secrecy in a world of concealed weapons. Then the deadlock might be resolved. If Russia accepts the three basic propositions listed above, the most sinister apprehensions might be ruled out; and the obstacles to agreement be reduced to proportions that might yield to persistence and good faith.

On the Russian side, if a *modus vivendi* is reached, there is some chance that time may relax the rigor of their control of information, allowing the people to be reached by more facts about the outside world, which would also mean fewer propaganda lies about it. There is then a chance that contacts, plus the logic of events that do not go quite in accord with the Marxian bible, might stimulate the critical faculties of the Russian people to question such dogmas as the one that our system is bound to wage offensive war against theirs. Having introduced general literacy, as a necessary means to the spreading of communist doctrine, it would be remarkable if all their precautions could succeed in permanently preventing the next stage: namely, the development of some degree of critical judgment on the part of the reader. While history does not repeat itself exactly, it is worth remembering that the art of printing in Europe ushered in the Protestant Reformation.

With time, prosperity and safety—which every sane American must wish for the Russian people from the bottom of his heart— the rigor of the dictatorship could soften, letting the ideas of the people take more effect. In fact, it seems likely that the present repression is bound to wear itself out in time: not because the millennial stage is reached where the state is expected to "wither away," but because the repression involves the sort of strain which neither repressor nor repressed will endure permanently, when the initial stage of revolutionary *sturm und drang* is passed. But this wearing out process may not happen soon enough to save the world.

Among things that might take some effect, the most boldly constructive is probably the project of the American Friends' Service Committee which, in addition to "work camps" actually provided for in Poland, Finland, Italy, Germany and other countries, has an unfulfilled project for such a unit in the Ukraine. Its potential effect has, of course nothing to do with "appeasement" of the Kremlin, but hinges on friendly contacts and discussion with the people of the region. Since such contacts appear now to be more rigorously tabooed than ever, the prospects of gaining Soviet consent do not appear bright, though if anyone could win an exemption from this policy, the Quakers presumably could. Admittedly it is a gamble against heavy odds; but unlike political concessions for purposes of "appeasement," it involves no yielding of the values we are trying to defend. From such contacts we might learn some things to our advantage, if we are open-minded enough, including a more objective view of the Russian people than we get from the acts and pronouncements of public characters, bound to conformity with official policy and orthodoxy.

Last, but not least, a crucial goal in the next crucial few years is to keep the United Nations in being, as active and strong as possible and ready to enlarge its powers the moment that the attitudes of the dominant nations will permit. It is the only body comprehensive enough to afford a basis for the ultimate collective security of the world. But the price of this comprehensiveness is lack of present power to control any major aggressor, and this is its basic dilemma. This means, necessarily, a double policy. It means building up all agencies and activities which Russia has not boycotted, including the settlement of those "minor" disputes which can so easily spread. And it means that, where other methods have to be followed, to meet vital needs, every effort possible should be made to pursue them in harmony with the United Nations, to the end that it may gain strength from any success they may be able to achieve, rather than being weakened by it, and may grow toward a condition in which it may be able itself to do the things for which it was designed. This is easy to say, and heartbreakingly difficult to achieve.

In the meantime, we must maintain negotiations. We must cultivate the fine art of wrangling with Russians without letting it degenerate into art for art's sake. We must meet both hard bargaining and obstructionism. Recognizing that objections may be made for filibustering purposes, we must still look for the occasional valid point, and give it due consideration. Resenting torrents of false accusation and abuse, we must neither ignore it nor respond in kind—that would be "untactful"—but refute it patiently, without letting this divert us from getting on with the job in hand.

6. ECONOMIC REHABILITATION OF EUROPE

There can be no serious question that aid to Europe should be sufficient to meet the requirements of rehabilitation and that countries should be expected to do their utmost to help themselves and to help one another by opening trade for the freer exchange of essential goods. This will not fully compensate for the reduced volume of trade with eastern Europe, but it will help. Sixteen countries have chosen participation, in the face of Soviet propaganda against the plan, including sweeping accusations of our intent to use it to rule the world, and the attempt to blame us because eastern Europe refused the invitation.[1] Their choice took some courage. It remains that they should not be disappointed in any proper and essential expectations.

[1] Cf. Stalin's interview with British members of Parliament, referred to above.

As to whether the offer should remain open to all European countries, that is by now presumably a closed issue. More difficult is the question whether we should strictly refrain from exercising any pressure as to the methods by which countries shall choose to put their own houses in order. We should not use such pressure to promote our own direct commercial or industrial interests, nor to force countries to maintain the particular degree of "capitalism" which we prefer to maintain in this country. But if obsolescent reactionary elements are in power, our aid will go to them and tend to maintain them, unless we violate the principle of non-interference and throw our weight in favor of liberalizing reforms. Furthermore, if communist sabotage of the "Marshall plan" becomes very formidable, in the shape of political strikes and disorders or worse, severe repressive measures may be the only alternative, bringing the situation uncomfortably close to that of Italy after the first World War, out of which Fascism arose in 1919–1922. Here and there, locally, aid may even be captured and exploited by communist elements.

If there is any way out of this group of dilemmas, it hinges on something basically simple, underlying the complications. If the decisive majority of the people, in countries cooperating with us, think that their government represents their true interests better than Moscow does, they will not choose Moscow. Then Moscow can win only by force of some sort; and the question becomes one of protection against force, and the methods of minority control that are founded on it, in such a baffling variety of ways. This means that governments must represent the interests of the masses of their own people; a government that itself represents a repressive and exploitative minority will not have the basis necessary to succeed in resisting the repressive minority of the left. It will aid communist parties to gain willing votes by promising the masses better treatment, and charging us with perpetuating their exploitation. If we are led to interfere in domestic matters, it should be in the interest of reforms offering the masses hope of real improvement. Communist offers of land to peasants may be specious, but are concretely appealing. Soviet propaganda cannot be appeased, but receptiveness may be reduced. All of this means further that administration of American aid will call for more than administrative efficiency; it will call for the highest grade of political wisdom the country can muster.

Rehabilitation includes Germany; a hopeless and chaotic Germany will wreck the rest of the program. Germany must import food, because it lacks area enough to grow its own. To do this it must export nonfood products, and to do this it must have industries capable of producing a surplus not mortgaged to reparations. This could be harmonized with protecting France against German rearmament. It is difficult to see how it could be harmonized with accepting the Russian terms for the unification of Germany. This leaves an unsolved impasse.

The economic effects on this country of aiding Europe, while substantial, take second place. In the early stages, the aid tends to slow down our own postwar rebuilding and restocking, which may be a blessing in disguise by spreading the process out, and preventing it from leading to a sudden and severe glut. It obviously increases particular shortages and inflationary pressures, which is unpleasant, but not radically dangerous, if we use reasonable good sense in dealing with it. Later, if our own postwar boom tapers off, aid to Europe may be a welcome addition to declining domestic demand. This would not be likely to mean exporting our unemployment to Europe, since Europe would probably still have a labor shortage. If we were to suffer a really disastrous economic collapse, as the Soviets hope and predict, the burden of European aid might come to seem prohibitive on financial grounds; but we have it on Eugene Varga's authority that there is no apparent likelihood of this in the first postwar decade.

The serious test will come later, when the various temporary postwar stimuli have exhausted themselves. If the export surplus brought about by the "Marshall plan" aid comes to an end abruptly, this could give our economy a rude jolt. If it tapers off gradually, still we should need to be adjusting our system to maintain a high level of production and employment without the stimulus of an abnormally large export surplus. That is the real test of whether we can overcome the "laws of capitalist development" which Marxism sees as driving us to ultimate collapse. More accurately, it sees them as so weakening us that the ultimate collapse can be brought about by a push from the organized comrades.

7. OUR OWN HOUSE IN ORDER

Meanwhile, we face the task of strengthening democracy at home. And one thing we need to learn from the rest of the world, including Russia, is to question our inherited illusion that a juxtaposition of undisciplined private purposes, driving in all directions, can make up a society. While we renew our appreciation of the worth of freedom, as we see what happens when it is lost, we need to understand also its seamy side: the evils about which we cannot afford to be complacent. These include not only tangible economic shortcomings, but the worship of quantity, the pursuit of sensation, of "power without purpose," of materialism, and the debunking bent carried to destructive lengths. One of the keys of democracy is expressed in such phrases as "Oh, yeah," or "sez you," epitomizing the right to be outspokenly and impudently skeptical. This serves to discredit outworn myths and conventional canons. When it runs wild, it can end by discrediting all essential values, and producing an uprooted mentality and moral chaos.

One of our most crucial tasks in saving our civilization is to supply the lack which all this indicates: to find for the common man a feeling of his place in the whole community and a sense of common purpose. This may be impossible, short of outright collectivism. One wonders if any great people, in an age of scientific skepticism, has ever developed, voluntarily and democratically, such morale and discipline as we now need. But it is unquestionably necessary if freedom and democracy are to survive, and it seems about equally necessary under private enterprise or collectivism. More tangibly, it is necessary to the task of making our economic system work, with a maximum reliance on voluntary action, well enough to maintain its continuity of evolutionary development, and avoid a violent break.

The Soviets count on our system collapsing, and barring a change of policy, they will do their best to promote that end. And their best can be far from negligible, in a structure of organized and conflicting power groups, forced to find new ways of working together in a new power balance, with both internal and external peace precarious. It is not a simple contest of ideas as to what is the best system, as some idealists seem to think. That would be the democratic way, where people argue openly and sincerely for what they want and believe, and the minority accepts the judgment of the majority to the extent of giving it a fair chance to make its ideas work. That is democratic morality, for which revolutionary morality has no place, except, apparently, in the secret deliberations of the fourteen men who determine Soviet high policy. They disagree, until the final verdict is reached, then all support it.

By way of contrast, the tactics of a communist fifth column in a democratic country may be illustrated by the methods of minority control used inside trade unions, and in capturing liberal organizations and perverting them. These have been analyzed, and are fairly well understood. Such tactics are all the more dangerous because they are extreme forms of things that happen daily in normal democratic procedures, and some of them are even defensible within narrow and ill-defined limits, as informal ways in which minorities may legitimately be protected against majority tyranny. When a few carry a disproportionate part of the work of running an organization, it is commonplace that they have a disproportionate say as to how it is run. Within the basic general purposes of the institution, this is legitimate; communist fifth columns merely extend it to perverting that basic purpose.

When a minority feels that something is vital to its essential interests, and the majority has nothing equally vital at stake, the minority may strive to give their inferior numbers superior weight by wearing their opponents down in argument. But the filibuster, if used often or in defense of anything but important rights, is recognized as an abuse of democratic procedures. It is also an abuse when supposedly respectable politicians confuse issues, sabotage one another's measures or weaken unity by deliberately stirring dissension.

We have private and lawless violence at times, but not systematically wielded at the behest of the rulers of the state. Our official government pronouncements sometimes do violence to truth, generally in minimizing internal dissension or the extent of military disasters. But Mr. Byrnes or others retain freedom to expose them later, and this keeps such tactics within rather narrow bounds. Fifth columns merely carry all these abuses to the ultimate degree, and use them for the perversion of the basic purposes of the institution and the ultimate enslavement of the majority.

Just as totalitarians are teaching us afresh the value of liberty by destroying it, so they are teaching us the requisites for democracy by showing us what happens when they are sabotaged with ruthless completeness. In each case, lesser abuses which we tend to tolerate are exposed as evils, as we see what they lead to if used in this total fashion. In much the same way, insanity or neurosis is made up of defective traits which every normal person has. The difference between the normal and the psychopathic is that the normal person holds them within bounds, while the psychopathic lets them go to harmful excess. We have to keep our democracy from passing the psychopathic boundary. If this means sitting up all night through a sabotaged union meeting, the price is no heavier than Americans often pay for tickets to a world series baseball game. Unions were taking action on this danger, even before the Taft-Hartley Act added its ban on union officials with avowed membership in the Communist party. The outcome depends more on unions' continued vigilance than on legal provisions.

If critics point to imperfections in our liberty or democracy, the citizen can make one fairly simple test. He can search the critics' propaganda to see if they are trying to give us more and better liberty and democracy, or to trick us into giving up what we have, like a man who jumps into the water because the rain is wetting his coat. That is the logic of insanity, but this does not guarantee that it will not prevail, in the kind of social chaos which revolution deliberately promotes. Remembering that freedom, like wetness, is a matter of degree, the degree we have is high enough to be invaluable, aside from the fact that it is combined with material plenty.

It is good Marxian doctrine that a social system does not disappear until it has developed its full potentialities. Has ours done that? The answer depends on whether we develop our potentialities for making it work. If we do that, its greatest potentialities lie ahead, for a people that can rise to the present "challenge." Our capacity so to rise has not been proved; we may succeed or we may fail.

The job of the forces of totalitarianism is to pervert and sabotage the machinery and the morals of democracy. Our internal job is first to re-educate ourselves in the essentials of democracy, and to be willing to pay the proverbial price. Second, it is to make both our political and our economic system work— something neither will do automatically—in the face of inherent difficulties, increased by skilled efforts at sabotage. With an economic system which sensible people should prefer to the totalitarian, and a political system which registers what the people prefer, totalitarian minorities should have ceased to be a serious danger.

8. WHAT IS AT STAKE

There is more at stake than our own fate. We can hardly claim to be the best example of democracy, but at present we are the strongest; and if we go down, it is hard to see where the lights can stay lit. One of the things that is peculiarly disturbing in the thought of an all-embracing Soviet world empire, is the prospect that the only recorded history of the world, from dinosaurs to commissars, would be set in the mold of Stalinist orthodoxy. Something would have perished, more important than cities or armies.

Not by our special merit, but by the accidents of history, we have been "set as a tower and fortress" among the peoples.[1] The position is thoroughly uncomfortable and thoroughly dangerous; to let it feed our pride would be evidence, not only of a vainglorious spirit, but of lack of common sense. It is easier to become discouraged as to our ability to match the requirements of the emergency. But because we have no right to fail, we cannot afford either pride or discouragement, only dedication and unlimited hard work, guided by a searching study of the problem which discards prejudice and examines every constructive possibility. It is a superhuman task; but that is not to be dwelt on; because the survival of some of the values we identify with civilization depends on the free countries' collectively seeing it through.

[1] To paraphrase Jeremiah 6, 27. Jeremiah was not a cheerful prophet.

OBJECTIVES WITHIN OUR ECONOMY

1. FREEDOM FOR WHAT?

In the first lectures, we dealt with the defense of basic freedoms against a world threat. These basic freedoms are personal and political, and I shall take for granted that we want them. There may be some economic freedoms that are basic, too, but just how much they include is not certain. That is precisely the main debatable issue between democratic socialists and advocates of private enterprise. The basic personal and political freedoms include freedom to decide the question what sort of an economic system we want, with what kind of a balance between freedom and control, between private and public operation, between the kind of freedom involved in private business enterprise and freedoms of other sorts.

That is democracy, and it imposes its conditions on these lectures. It means that the lecturer is under an obligation to report faithfully what "we," the American people, think are desirable ends, and to do his best not to switch from "we" to "I" without due notice. That still leaves him a considerable margin of discretion. The Centralia mine disaster does not compel him to conclude that Americans approve of the killing of a hundred and eleven miners, as part of the cost of mining coal, because they tolerated the tangle of interlocking responsibilities that led to this disaster. What the people negligently do, or tolerate, is no good index of what they would approve of, if consequences and alternatives were made plain, and attention were focussed on them. Often we just don't know what we are doing, and when we find out, we change. The lecturer can fairly claim the privilege of forecasting some of those changes, while still speaking in the first person plural, not singular.[1]

There are some things about an economic system that we like or dislike for their own sakes; but for the most part we ask what it does for us. What do we want it to do for us? What is the crucial product by which an economic system can be tested, and a good system can be identified?

The most important product is people: good and healthy people, living various kinds of good lives, exercising and developing their capacities, protected against crippling ills, and having the kinds of relations to one another that constitute a good and healthy society. Incidentally, these activities and protections need to be implemented with material means, goods and services, including the kinds people buy in markets and kinds they get in other ways. And, to produce more goods, we introduce methods that change people's activities and human relations—perhaps for the better and perhaps for the worse. The increased supply of goods may not be the most important effect, but merely the one easiest to measure.

[1] With regard to the principle that science, as science, should not make value-judgments, economics is in a peculiar position, being, traditionally at least, a science of values. Without entering into the dispute as to whether ethics may or may not be scientific; for economics it is possible, and traditionally fitting, to maintain neutrality between values, though it cannot, in the nature of the case, maintain aloofness. The above paragraph is an attempt to express the nearest approach to neutrality that is feasible for economics. As I have already indicated, the economist's favorite refuge—accepting the verdict of the market—is a false neutrality, since the market has its own strong biases, promoting and protecting some kinds of values and relatively neglecting others.

For particular alternatives *as the economist sees them*, he can almost never find a popular verdict representing a valid judgment as to which is preferable —the economist would not be an economist unless he saw the consequences and alternatives in a light different from that in which they appear to the general public. So the choice he sees is not the same one the public sees, and he must try to judge what verdict the public's *values* would dictate, if they had the economist's view of the *consequences* and *alternatives*.

It constitutes what we call "prosperity," but prosperity in that sense is a means, not an end. Economists are supposed to forget that fact, when they are busy being economists; but forgetting is seldom a virtue.

The topic first suggested for these lectures stressed prosperity for America. But that did not seem the most appropriate keynote in a world that is literally cold, ragged and hungry, struggling to reconstitute the disrupted basis of its economic life. Of course, an economic collapse in this country would be a world calamity; therefore, in the long run, it is our duty to maintain our prosperity. Meanwhile it is our duty to share it. On second thought, the Latin derivation of the word "prosperity" suggested a less materialistic meaning than we usually attach to it. "Pro" is used presumably in the sense of "favorable to" or "responsive to," and "spero" means "to hope." In that light, the word means "responsive to one's hopes": an America whose future may be made in the image of one's hopes, not one's fears, doubts or discouragements. That would be an inspiring subject to discuss.

But, using the word in its usual sense, is it strange for an economist, in his professional capacity, to question "prosperity" as a primary objective? I agree that we must be prosperous; the kind of virtues, the kind of good life, which we must aim at, are those consistent with material prosperity, whether that is an advantage or a handicap. But when the question is whether civilization can survive—whether man is about to destroy himself, or, short of that, whether the qualities we think most essential can go on living in the world—it seems hardly fitting to get overexcited about prosperity in the sense of bigger and better movie houses, streamlined autos with more gadgets, or even more bathtubs. One might put it in this way: given a country with all the technical power and capability we have, if we are not prosperous, there must be something rotten in our state. We want a sound state and a sound people; if we have these, under existing conditions, material prosperity will be an inevitable by-product.

But the requirements of a sound state are broader and deeper.

An economic system is an instrument—our instrument. We shall see in a moment that it is something more, but it is that. As an instrument, it is to be judged by how well it serves our ends. So the first question to ask, logically, is: "What are our ends? What do we want, or what should we want?"[1] Some of you may have studied economics enough to know that it does not go at the question in that way. It studies the mechanism as an instrument for serving unspecified ends-in-general; which means in practice whatever ends the mechanism happens to be adapted to serve. And some economists have ingenious ways of proving, to their own satisfaction, that economics must be a science of means without reference to ends, and that consideration of ends, such as I am proposing, is unscientific.

Don't let them confuse you. What that logically leads to is judging the system by *its* ends, not ours; by the ends it is best adapted to serve, those it tends to promote and cultivate. This tendency was too strong during the nineteenth century, both in practice and in theory. If carried too far, it means that we let the system be our master, not our servant; we surrender to its natural tendencies. For it does have tendencies; it is not merely an inanimate instrument, it is one of those social institutions which C. H. Cooley called "impersonal forms of life"; and its tendencies act like purposes distinct from those of the individuals who compose it.[2]

There is nothing mystical about this. One man does something for a purpose of his own. This affects the interests of several others and they react, protecting their interests and partially defeating the first man's purpose. He responds; and by this time a wider circle of interests is affected. The circles of response keep spreading, till the resultant is something different from what any

[1] I have touched on this question in Alternative to Serfdom, pp. 10–11. For the opposite view, see Lionel Robbins, The Nature and Significance of Economic Science, 2nd ed., pp. 136–43.

[2] C. H. Cooley, Social Process, p. 4 ff.

one of them intended, and different from what all together would have voted for, if they had had the chance. It may be worse or better, or it may be better in some respects and worse in others. One of the great things that are happening, in this great age in which we live, is a struggle to convert the free economy from something that responds mainly to its own unplanned tendencies, into something animated by purposes: purposes into which its members can and do enter. This is both a promise and a danger: a promise for obvious reasons and a danger because it has not been proved that we are competent to steer society to sound and safe goals, and there is evidence pointing in the other direction.

Conscious social objectives have not before been needed in the same form and sense, participated in by the many. That comes when the many gain power. In earlier times, only the powerful few have consciously shaped their world, while the masses acted under kingly or ecclesiastical authority. The medieval world was almost static in its social framework and its economic techniques; and in the minds of many, it served mainly as an antechamber to the next world.

Now we focus differently. In the first place, we focus on this world. There is a next world, vastly more important than this, whether in the old sense or not, whether an afterworld or an earthly posterity. But for the next world we are surest of, the key is what we make of this one, not for ourselves, but for our descendants. It is not what we get out of it for ourselves—that we can neither take with us nor leave for our heirs. It is something more enduring.

In the second place, we are all free to participate, according to our vision and grasp, in the decisions that shape what the enduring world is to be. We do not, as a people, lack power; a people with such power as we have needs most a supremely worth-while end to which to put it. Lacking this, mere power is the most dangerous thing in the world, whether in atom bombs or in the economic market place.

2. SOME RIVAL OBJECTIVES

Conscious objectives often center on ills we want to avoid. At present, we are a little troubled by a food shortage* (shortage, relative to the "effective demand" of the best fed people in the world), and shortages of steel and machinery (relative to the demand of a country more amply supplied than any other). We are concerned lest these aggravate an inflationary boom; and if the boom ends, we are concerned lest it bring depression and unemployment with it. Put in positive terms we want a fairly stable price level, and continuance of the highest national income, in terms of goods, that any country has ever enjoyed, plus an increase as existing shortages are made good.

Our material objectives are not modest, and they should not be; but on two conditions. One is that we remember that material income is only a means, and that worth-while ends to put it to are more important. The other is that we temper our particular aspirations with a sense of what is attainable without sacrificing to one aim others that are more important. Economics teaches that single aims have their price, and the price must be considered in deciding how far it is wise or prudent to push them. To set up any one absolute and unconditional goal is dangerous. The task of framing social objectives is to fit these single aims into a consistent and coherent picture of something that can, within the limits of human foresight, be regarded as reasonably attainable. Having stressed the need of looking at ends, we may take up next the problem of balancing ends against one another.

We want goods, marketable goods; but that does not define what we want them for. They free us from privation and suffering, they furnish the means of health and strength and, at the stage of plenty we have now reached, they implement our freedom for a wide variety of activities, personal and social. As we get more and more prosperous, added income goes less and less into meeting physical necessities, and more and more into implementing activities, good and bad, wise and foolish. They represent freedom to be and to do what we want to be and do.

But if this kind of freedom is what we really get out of more goods of the sort people buy in markets, it depends at least equally on community conditions, things that are not for sale in markets, but have to be won and preserved in other ways. It depends on mundane things like traffic rules, and on imponderables like human relations on the job, and the state of tolerant or intolerant feeling between classes. These are often unintended byproducts of the methods we follow to get cheap and plentiful goods—by-products, that is, from the standpoint of the motives that make things happen. From the standpoint of consequences to the community, these by-products are often more important than the supposed main product.

To state objectives in general terms is only a first step. We want goods, well-distributed, security, greater equality (of some sorts, especially "equal opportunity"), human rights, (including rights of group action), justice, jobs. At present, we want all these things under a system of "private enterprise." But as we move toward making these aims specific, conflicts appear and compromise becomes necessary. Goods are multiplied by mass production, but this interferes with the simple human contacts and relations on the job, which we regard as desirable. Private enterprise limits the supply of goods to what can be sold at profitable prices; raising the difficult question how far this is an expression of unavoidable natural limits on supply, and how far it results from institutions that might be changed. Complete freedom for business enterprise conflicts with various rights and freedoms of other parties. Freedom of business to organize in a monopolistic direction restricts the buyer's freedom to get the benefit of choice between competing sellers.

We could probably get "full employment" by reducing productivity and making ourselves poorer, or by a system of complete collectivism, neither of which would be welcome. If we want private enterprise and high productivity, what price in unemployment is it necessary to pay, what price are we willing to pay, and how far may the price be mitigated? Complete equality of opportunity turns out on examination to be impossible; but if we made this a paramount goal and were in dead earnest about it, one of the first things we should have to do would be to abolish the private family. A system of distribution that puts goods where they yield the greatest benefit means, to some, distribution according to need; but this would wipe out the most prevalent tangible incentives to increased output, and would conflict with those ideas of rights and justice which hold that reward should be according to performance. There is a place for both principles in our system; but the question how to fit them together is only one of many difficult problems we are now trying to work out.

3. WAYS OF ADJUSTING CONFLICTS OF OBJECTIVES: THE PRINCIPLE OF STRATEGIC DECISIONS

Where conflicts exist, the inevitable question is: how much of each objective are we going to keep? And the kinds of conflicts just outlined cannot be settled in the way economics likes best to settle conflicts of values. The conflicts it deals with most happily are those involved in budgeting a limited dollar income between different kinds of purchases; and here economics passes the onus on to the individual purchaser, and accepts his decision on how much to spend on one thing and how much on another. In these conflicts of social objectives, we have got to make the decision ourselves, by collective judgment, and it is not easy.

There are various ways of going at it. One is the way of "muddling through" and patching. As each discontent gets troublesome, we do enough about it to allay the immediate pressure of dissatisfaction without rousing more dissatisfaction in other quarters, and hope for the best. The result is piecemeal compromise, often without consistency and generally without long-run consideration of consquences, or of the total impact of the whole sequence of emergency repairs. In the kind of survey we are making here, we need more in the way of guiding philosophy and perspective.

One kind of philosophy, the conservative kind, judges a system by its own accepted values—always one or a few that are dominant at a particular time—thus automatically ratifying any biases the system may have, and tending to preserve them. If the system overemphasizes the freedoms of business enterprise, its articulate philosophy is likely to exaggerate this bias, making freedom the supreme criterion, though it will talk about freedom in general, not freedom for one class of interests. Then if one wants to justify measures limiting freedom in the interest of security, one has to go through the process of showing that security is, after all, a kind of freedom, as "liberal" philosophers are doing today. Thus philosophy can, somewhat awkwardly, circumvent the obstacles it has itself raised when it made one value supreme, and vindicate its right to consider different kinds of values. But the kinds of "freedom" remain qualitatively different; we are still trying to weigh incommensurables.

This kind of bias in favor of dominantly accepted values is hard to avoid, even for scholars who take in a fairly long historical perspective, and try to project the enduring trends of history, and to be guided by them. If one takes, for example, the period from the stirrings that presaged the Protestant Reformation to the end of the dominance of nineteenth-century ideas and practices (possibly 1914—the precise date is immaterial), one has an epoch of about four centuries, comprising most of "modern" times, during which the dominant civilization was that of western Europe, and its dominant motif was liberty. By comparison, the decades of the rise of totalitarianism can easily seem a short, though violent, eddy in the main current.

Nevertheless, I do not believe those four centuries are a safe guide to the long-run trend of history. Before that, the discipline of the Catholic Church overshadowed the movement toward liberty, and during the "modern" period, liberty was growing at the expense of community coherence and discipline, until it went beyond a healthy balance. Needless to say, I am not going to speak of totalitarianism as the "wave of the future." But I suspect that the theme of history, over a longer period than those four "libertarian" centuries, is the quest for a balance between liberty and this other element—call it a sense of belonging to something bigger than one's self, and the psychological and material security that goes with this when it is placed at the service of democracy and humanity, not tyranny and inhuman ideology. The nineteenth century upset the balance in favor of excessive liberty, totalitarianism is punishing us by upsetting things in the opposite direction. The balance that can save us remains to be found.

This same method, of setting up one value as absolute and supreme, may be applied to values which the system tends to neglect; then it becomes radical instead of conservative. In either case, the corrective is not likely to be applied until too late to avoid the sacrifice of greater to lesser values.

Over against these is the method of weighing particular alternative policies, and the price that has to be paid for each item of gain, and deciding whether the probable gain is worth the probable price, and whether some other combination of policies will work out a preferable result. The difficulty with this method is that the possible alternatives and combinations are so numerous that the mind is overwhelmed. The problem would baffle the genius of a chess master.

There is one way of simplifying it enough to make it reasonably manageable. To give it a pretentious name, one may call it the "method of strategic decisions." I will state it abstractly, and then try to clarify it with a few illustrations. It consists of starting with key decisions about which there is a minimum of doubt, and examining their necessary consequences, good and bad, desired and undesired. If, after such an examination, the decision still seems to stand, we accept whatever undesirable features appear to be unavoidable. We treat them as the price that has to be paid for something that is worth the price, and dismiss them as liabilities against the system as a whole. These strategic decisions are of different sorts. It is possible that some conditions may have to be accepted, simply because they represent changes that are historically irreversible—we cannot turn the clock back fifty or a hundred years. Some are inevitable because anything else would be administratively impracticable, others because American values are what they are.

This method is consistent with accepting prevailing values, but not with accepting everything that is done in their name when the authorities are "muddling through" with patchwork solutions of particular crises, or when many groups of reformers are each intent on curing a different particular evil. The method calls for an appraisal of consequences that is as far-sighted as humanly possible, and for an attempt to estimate the total impact of all the measures that may be taken.

4. ACCEPTING THE CONSEQUENCES OF MASS PRODUCTION AND GROUP POWER

First, let us look at some of the changes that are historically irreversible and follow out their main consequences. This is a different country and a different world from the one in which my father began his studies in Amherst, just after the Civil War, and was encouraged by President Julius Seelye to make the investigation of economic problems his lifework. We could not go back if we wanted to, and we ought not to want to. Strong labor organizations and huge industrial units create problems, but they are not only inevitable, they are necessary to do things we cannot do without. What we do must be done in this setting; the objectives we set must be such as will fit into this framework. Any aims inconsistent with these primary conditions are visionary wishful thinking.

Try to imagine going back to a system in which workers deal as individuals with large-scale employers, leaving their human rights at the mercy of arbitrary discipline and discharge, and wages and hours subject to the rigors of unmitigated competition. Something like that might possibly happen under a totalitarian system, because one of the first things such a system does, along with destroying freedom of the press, is to subjugate unions. But if basic political freedoms are preserved, they will sustain the right of labor to organize. Or if this right were abolished, (taking us back to the first decades of the nineteenth century) it would have to be recreated— preferably within such limits as experience might suggest to prevent the growth of an irresponsible labor tyranny, but leaving room for the development of real strength.

Or we can imagine going back to a system in which a multitude of competing business units pursue their own profits, using such methods as small business units have the wit to devise, and with no community responsibilities except respecting legal rights of property and person, fulfilling contracts and refraining from getting together to extinguish competition. That also, besides being impossible, would not be a good system. Productivity would be limited, and this would limit our prosperity, though not seriously. But local employers, hard-pressed by competition in the sale of their products, would often have enough control of their local labor market to make their workers pay for their own inefficiency by accepting substandard conditions. So competition might be harder on specific groups of unfortunate workers than on the employers as a whole. Such a system might create less unemployment in time of depression than the system of great corporate enterprise has done in the last twenty years, though of that one cannot be certain. But it would be shot through with abuses and injustices, and we should not let it stay without trying to change it. Perhaps, if we could go back to it, and start over, with the memory of our first attempt to help, we should do better the second time, and then again, perhaps we should not.

The right of workers to organize is not merely a means of protecting and furthering their interests in wages, hours and other matters, important as that is. It is really an end in itself, a spontaneous tendency of people of the same occupation to express their "consciousness of kind."[1] It means group power, and power can be abused. In the political arena, the same tendency brings "pressure group government," which the New Deal deliberately fostered. This probably deserves most of the bad things that are said about it by old-fashioned liberals; but one can see now that the liberal's ideal had its defects, too.

It held, correctly, that minority groups of producers should not exploit the majority; but this led to the erroneous conclusion that the interests of producers should be dominated by the interests of consumers, these being the interests which the majority has in common. In the same way, competitive markets tend to subordinate producers' interests to consumers', until life, health, employment and human relations on the job, are all at the mercy of an impersonal market and imperfect and lopsided competitive forces. This is, in its way, about as wrong as the excesses of "pressure groups." From this standpoint, the New Deal was a recognition, necessarily imperfect, of neglected values. Something of the sort, in some form, was probably necessary, as well as inevitable.

All this means power in the hands of organized groups: both economic power and political power used for economic ends. It means that we accept this and take the necessary consequences. Perhaps it is time to revise Lord Acton's famous dictum, which may have been overworked of late: "Power tends to corrupt, and absolute power corrupts absolutely." There is a deal of truth in this, but just how much? Perhaps the opposite truth is equally pertinent: "Impotence degrades or corrodes. Absolute impotence corrodes dangerously." Or if one prefers psychological language, one can say: "Frustration breeds neuroses." Both Lord Acton's statement and its converse are half-truths. It would be absurd to

[1] The phrase is Franklin H. Giddings.' As to this application of the idea, cf. Frank Tannenbaum, "The Social Function of Trade Unions," Pol. Sci. Quar., June, 1947, pp. 161–194.

assume that every judge or official is corrupted because he has power, and equally absurd to claim that totalitarian tyranny always succeeds in degrading its victims. But it takes an Epictetus to bring great philosophy out of slavery, and it takes a Booker Washington to say: "No one shall degrade me enough to make me hate him." The result seems to rest with the individual's perspective, enlightenment and moral fibre. Great power, or great impotence in face of arbitrary and unjust power, both call for supreme character to respond constructively. Moderate power, and limits on it, are regular parts of the situation in which normal character should develop. In economic life, the theory of the overruling power of "economic law" was a theory of the powerlessness of the human agents to alter the inevitable outcome. This theory of impotence does not fit the present facts. What we have to evolve is a system that will be workable, starting with great corporate enterprises and labor unions, both possessing a great deal of power to protect themselves from competitive forces, and government agencies exercising increasing power over the outcome.

Under such conditions, a good outcome requires limitations on arbitrary power, and responsible use of the power that remains. This will succeed in proportion as the limitations are voluntarily accepted, and worked out in the light of an understanding of the situations and needs of all parties concerned, and the requirements of voluntary working together. So the strategic fact of the inevitability of group power has led us to what seems the most basic economic principle of the present age and the visible future. It is that the amount of freedom we can keep is limited and measured by the degree of responsibility with which economic power is exercised, and limitations upon it are voluntarily accepted.[1] This has moral implications, but I have tried to formulate it as a thoroughly objective statement of cause and effect.[2] The necessity it expresses is rooted in modern techniques, and it holds true,

[1] Cf. Alternative to Serfdom, esp. pp. 3–4 & Chap. V.

[2] For any precise methodologists who may read this, it refers to the kind of functional relationship commonly spoken of as "cause and effect," by the unsophisticated public.

whether the system that applies these techniques is labelled "capitalism" or "socialism." It seems to be as valid a generalization from observable fact as other generalizations that have been widely accepted as scientific economic laws. And it gives us one of our most fundamental objectives.

Irresponsible use of economic power leads either to chaos or coercion. As I have said elsewhere, a state cannot surrender to chaos, but it may lose its liberal character in combatting it.[1] So the objective is to establish ways of acting which may relieve our government from facing this hard alternative. This has to be done in face of sabotage by a revolutionary minority whose aim is precisely the opposite, and which is expert at disguising its real objectives, and gaining power by using it for normal ends, until the time for revolutionary use is ripe. When it comes to action, the crucial question is one of kind and degree. How much turbulence can the system assimilate? How much coercion, of what kinds, can it tolerate without losing its basic character? How much responsibility, of what sorts, will it take to prevent either turbulence or coercion from going beyond the tolerable limits? In the last analysis, only experience will give the answer.

A realistic objective must recognize that perfection is out of reach, and is therefore dangerous to insist on, since it may lead to demands for change which carry no rational prospect of improvement. The aim is that organized groups, of capital or labor, should have powers that can and will be used for salutary reduction of insecurity, and that these should be supplemented by public action in the fields of social insurance and stabilization of employment, while the use of these powers to the twin ends of monopolistic exploitation and inflation should be kept to a minimum which the system can safely tolerate.

5. CONSEQUENCES OF ACCEPTING EVOLUTIONARY CHANGE

So far, we have been following out the consequences of one "strategic decision": the acceptance of organized economic power.

[1] See Alternative to Serfdom, pp. 25–6, 143.

Now we may break into this endless network of relationships at another point. It seems safe to say that we choose evolutionary change, as preferable to abrupt revolution, especially if the latter is violent. At present, we choose to maintain a system of private enterprise, but not unchanged. The idea that the institution as a whole is on trial is growing, though not prevailingly accepted. What is prevailingly accepted is a considerable need for change: enough to make it seem that when we say we choose to maintain private enterprise, we are really saying that we choose to let change come in the evolutionary way. It means working by trial and error within the framework of the institution and not pushing change faster than the system can adapt itself to it. If there is some maximum limit on the amount of change the system can stand and maintain its health, even if given plenty of time to adjust, then evolution means not straining it beyond this limit.

This does not preclude the possibility of ultimately going farther; but it means that if such a change should come, it would come by the gradual development of other kinds of agencies, taking over more and more functions. They would need to learn how to do it without subverting the health of the private agencies, and the private agencies on their side would need to be willing to do some adjusting. In short, it means a "mixed system," with a gradual change in the proportions of the mixture, until—if private enterprise is to give way to collectivism—the public sector might be in a position to take over the major economic functions without shock. One of the things that would need to be settled in the meantime is the question of how far government can go toward becoming the sole economic employer without fatally weakening the independent status of the citizen which is the necessary foundation of political self-government. But all this is something we shall not need to face soon; perhaps not in the present generation.

Nearly everyone will admit that historical change does not stand still; but most of us will conveniently forget this unless somebody forces us to face unmistakable evidence of the changes that are going on around us. The above represents a serious effort to interpret the real meaning of the actual prevalent American attitude which lies, more than half unconsciously, beneath this more superficial tendency to forget the endlessness of change. This deeper attitude would reveal itself in action from time to time, as issue after issue has to be dealt with. It leaves room for wide divergence of view as to how far change should go, and even as to the direction particular changes should take. Once more, the boundaries at any time can be set only by experience. But to avoid mistakes that would be irrevocable, in the process of "trial and error," experience should be guided by a wise alertness for symptoms of impaired health and vigor in the system.

Among the many lines of possible change which may test our capacity for evolutionary adjustment, outstanding ones include the great question already discussed, of the limits on the exploitive powers of organized groups, of capital or labor, by voluntary or compulsory methods, and the establishment of a balance between freedom and security. In the remaining lectures, we shall go into more specific questions of ways and means. We shall not come out with a detailed and final blueprint; but in a democratic society, that is not to be expected.

6. IMAGINARY RECONSTRUCTION AS AN ANALYTICAL DEVICE

So far, we have been accepting what seem to be the main conditioning trends of history; and this may leave an uneasy sense that we are acquiescing in things merely because they exist, though they might not be able to stand the test of rational appraisal. As a check on this, it may be worth-while to adopt the fiction that we are starting a new society, and to look at a few of the strategic decisions we should have to make. This may give some slight indication of what general features of our system will stand a rational test. It may point to some features that any system is bound to include, and others that American values dictate.

The operation is, of course, only an analytical device. Actually, in trying to modify our society, we carry our existing house on our backs, and cannot escape from it without terrific penalties. And if we were really to be setting up a new state, it would have to start young and grow to maturity, carrying the remains of its past self with it at every stage. Each stage will dictate its own characteristic ways of thinking, acting and organizing. If America in 1789 could have foreseen the atomic age, it could not then have organized for it; and now that the atomic age is here, the relics of 1789 and 1865 remain to plague it. It took inspired compromise to set up a system as flexibly adaptable as ours has proved to be. But with this warning, we may try the experiment.

7. POLICY AS TO CONSUMERS' FREE CHOICE, AND CONSEQUENCES

To pick a starting point—not quite at random—what shall we choose to do about consumers' free choice? Obviously, we shall give it wide scope, in ordinary goods for private use, but not in everything. Any conceivable system would do that, short of one in which the entire population is converted to the status of an army at war. This in itself carries far-reaching consequences. It means that people receive generalized purchasing power—in other words, money of some sort—and buy things in markets of some sort, at prices, and choose whether to buy one thing or another with a view to desire, quality and price.

Obviously, also, we shall not leave individual consumers entirely free to decide whether to buy narcotics, to quarantine contagious diseases, to attend school or not, to drink uninspected milk or eat in uninspected restaurants, or buy houses that might fall down or with wiring that might set them on fire. But, because American values are what they are, we shall leave them free to choose their reading matter and their church, if any, though soviet Russia treats these things differently. Aside from the precise points where we draw our lines, why do we draw the general kinds of lines we do? A full answer would fill volumes, but we can start with some things that are not the reason.

It is not because the individual infallibly chooses the best values. Our actual policy proves that we do not believe that. It is not because the individual chooses better than anyone else can choose for him. We prove our disbelief in that, too. We rightly judge that the "law" knows better than either the child or his parents whether or not he should go to school, the doctor knows better than the patient, the building code is a needed safeguard for the house-buyer against his own inability to see or judge the invisible items that enter into safe and durable construction. If the building code is too often perverted into an instrument to protect obsolete building methods and materials, or to favor Smith's product against Jones', the remedy is to reform the code, not abolish it.

The reason is not that there are no *scientific* grounds for over-ruling the customer's judgment or safeguarding it. A public health order and a rule against harmful adulterants have a scientific basis. It is fairly safe to assume that the normal buyer does not want his health injured; so the remaining question is one of fact, is this adulterant harmful? And we can get a better answer by hiring qualified people to make tests than by leaving it to the uninformed buyer, who may never know what hurt him.

Finally, our policy is not explained by any conviction that there is something so sacred about free individual choice that it must not be interfered with, right or wrong; or that people have a supreme right to make their own mistakes, and profit from them— if they can. This last principle breaks down where choices have irrevocable effects, and mistakes can be disastrous. But we are getting closer. People do have a right, which is supreme in a democracy, to *some* large area of free choice affecting their "way of living," and the form and color of their lives. On the other hand, they need protection from the impossible burden of a full application of the doctrine of *caveat emptor*, which would be crushing in an age when every year brings a bewildering assortment of new foods, medicines, gadgets and synthetic substitutes.[1]

Therefore, if we were drafting specifications for a new society, they would resemble the existing system at least in allowing scope for free individual choice that is large but not unlimited. The line might be drawn in different places, but it is safe to say that it would have a strong family resemblance to the lines we now draw. It would result from a great many particular decisions as to which values are the most important in many different specific cases. In making these decisions, the general theories we have been briefly reviewing will not help us much. They are all obsolete dogmas. They were born in times when the direction of change was different from that of today; and they furnished moral support for that direction of change, and agreed with the prevalent judgment in all the doubtful frontier cases, or most of them. But they were formulated by eighteenth-century theorists (and reformulated by their intellectual descendants): theorists with' a bent toward discovering universal natural laws of virtually-unqualified liberty. Be-

[1] The reader who is familiar with the literature of economic theory will recognize that the two preceding paragraphs constitute a denial of all the main assumptions that have been relied on by general or abstract theoretical economics dealing with utility or individual choice, from Bentham through Jevons and down to and including the assumptions which are implicit, though unavowed, in the currently-favored "indifference-curve" approach. In the fourth paragraph following, the position taken is at variance with the further view that economists must abjure all "interpersonal comparisons"—except, be it noted, those that are embodied in the existing distribution of incomes and existing purchases, which are largely made for family units, not for individuals. This appears to be a theorist's perversion of the valid principle that economists, as "scientists," should be neutral in these matters, and should be guided by actual prevailing valuations. In practice, this perversion leads to acceptance of market valuations, which are notoriously biased, in ways easily demonstrable. I maintain that there are other actual valuations which have more validity for this purpose, and that need to be taken into account by an economist who really wants to be neutral.

Obviously, detailed establishment of these negative criticisms would require a treatise, and would be out of place here. The main point that I am suggesting is a substitute method of dealing with these problems, which may not be easily recognized as "theory," but is based on theoretical analysis, and which, with all its indefiniteness, appears to come nearer the goal of objective neutrality which economists have set for themselves.

ware of such absolute universals, especially if you want change to come by evolutionary methods!

Obviously, there will be a sphere of liberty and spheres of control. And by our inherited division of labor between academic disciplines, economists are licensed to reason concerning the laws and mechanisms governing the things that are left in the sphere of free choice and exchange in markets, while political scientists can reason concerning the laws and mechanisms governing the action of public authority, and so presumably governing the things that are subject to its action. I say "presumably" because there seems to be a twilight zone where jurisdiction is in doubt. And this kind of departmentalized study may not tell much as to where the lines should be drawn between the sphere of liberty and that of control, or if it does, it is likely to point to traditional lines that have become obsolete. That is exactly the limitation of judgment we are trying to escape.

Presumably we shall leave individuals free to choose their clothes, furniture, color of fittings, make of automobile, if any, and similar things. Why? Because that kind of freedom means a lot to the individual, and is relatively unimportant to society. Our kind of society has nothing to gain by regimentation of such things, while the job of regimentation, and the resistance it would arouse, would be terrific. And we shall presumably leave adults free to choose their intellectual diet—presumably within some kind of limits barring the commercial exploitation of gross obscenity (a movable term) and barring propaganda which goes beyond the wide limits allowed in a society whose basic institution includes freedom to persuade one's fellow citizens that change is desirable. This reaches its limit where it creates a "clear and present danger" to the society, or tends directly to acts which the society regards as criminal or otherwise at war with its necessary conditions.

Within these wide limits, we shall let the consumer be the judge in the intellectual sphere, not because what he chooses is socially unimportant, as is the color of his socks, but for an almost opposite reason—because it is so basically important to a popularly-governed society that the individual be not subject to dictation in these matters. Most individuals will conform to some pattern or patterns: a fashion in socks, a demagogue in politics or a cult in philosophy or religion. The point is that, if a person chooses to change his pattern, nothing will happen to him beyond some possible private raillery or remonstrance. His freedom is real and important, even though he may not seem to be using it actively most of the time.

What of the basic economic necessities of life and health? These we shall surely not leave at the mercy of the individual's ability to secure and protect them in a devil-take-the-hindmost kind of market struggle. If he lacks the necessary means, we shall provide them, the only question being how much and under what conditions.[1] And if, having enough means, he lacks the facilities or the capacity to make safe choices among the goods that are offered him, we shall recognize that the community has proper grounds for doing something about that. If we were really making a fresh start, we should presumably see to it that the patent medicine business did not get the chance to grow up as it has. This might be incidental to a greatly enlarged and improved public health service.

In time of war or other extreme emergency, causing scarcity which threatens the necessities for large groups of the population, we shall ration the necessities of life on a basis of need. Crude as the available and administrable bases for gauging need must necessarily be, they are rightly preferred to what the uncontrolled forces of supply and demand would do in distributing these necessities, under such conditions. We shall be acting on the assumption that, with respect to these basic necessities, people's needs are approximately alike, with differences between adults and children, and between different occupations, which can be roughly estimated,

---

[1] Even the most extreme laissez-faire system had some organized poor-relief.

and which will bring about a more valid distribution of necessities than would result if provision were graded according to purchasing power. To sum up, there can be little doubt that we should approve some form of the principle of the "social minimum," with market forces allowed to determine distribution only above this minimum.

There is one further question. If we leave individuals free to choose what they will spend their incomes for, does that. mean that we leave them free to choose whether to spend or not to spend? That is not a purely individual concern, but one in which the community has a vital interest, since it helps to govern the volume of employment. On that matter, we shall probably try to influence their choice, but not dictate it. This is not for lack of a public interest in the result, but in the first place, because such dictation would be felt as inquisitorial tyranny and would hardly be administrable, and in the second place, there are. other and better ways of promoting more regular total spending.

Consumers' freedom of choice has further implications. A socialistic economy might produce goods in proportion to consumers' demand, or it might not. It would be under no compulsion to do so. To make consumers' choice the full governor of production, the consumer needs to be able to get someone to produce whatever he may want, without requiring government's consent: that is, his freedom needs to be complemented by a system of competitive private enterprise in production. This need not mean the American degree of emphasis on private enterprise, but the institution would have to be there, in working order as a going concern, even if only part of a "mixed system." Its minimum function would be to furnish an alternative to which the consumer could turn if socialized production were to grow either inert or autocratic in meeting consumers' legitimate desires, undertaking to rule him instead of being ruled by him, in those matters in which his interests are properly the primary concern.

8. FREE CHOICE OF OCCUPATIONS

This leads logically to one more kind of freedom: namely, free choice of occupations. In an industrialized economy, this involves freedom to move from place to place. Almost any economic system is bound to find it convenient to fill its various positions by inducing people to qualify for duties and accept them, rather than depending entirely on compulsory "selective service." Even Soviet Russia gives considerable scope to the voluntary principle, though using vastly more coercion than we should find tolerable. But this concerns choice among the occupations that the government chooses to allow or to establish. If the principle of freedom is to be allowed to decide *what occupations there shall be*, people must have the freedom to set up new occupations or to strike out new variants on old ones. This will not happen every day; but the difference between a system in which it is free to happen, and one in which it is not, is a tremendous difference.

This again requires a system including a good deal of free private enterprise, with the facilitating institutions and services that go with it, especially the ones that make it possible to acquire command of capital and give a new idea a trial. Not that every new occupation is set up in the field of private enterprise; some are generated in government service. The point is that, for effective freedom, both avenues need to be open.

9. EQUALITY

Flat equality of rewards has never been a part of the prevailing American ideal, and little time need be spent in disposing of it. The same is true of distribution solely according to need, with a qualification which will appear in a moment. Our actual standards are a curious and not too consistent mixture. By and large, we seem to want considerably less inequality than pure business principles would bring about. But we still recognize three reasons for a substantial amount of inequality of rewards. First, perhaps, is a general sense that it is fair that one who does more or better or more responsible and important work should get more for it. Second is a realization that differential rewards constitute one of the necessary incentives to induce people to extend themselves in productive effort. And third, there is realization that a scale of living considerably above the average is one of the necessary enabling conditions for accomplishing many of the highest-grade and most responsible kinds of work.

There are many individuals, and not all in "high grade" occupations, who will do good and sustained work because they are good and responsible workmen, interested in their jobs, or because they want to give the world their most appropriate and worth-while return for the living the world affords them. There are undoubtedly many to whom appreciation of their work (especially from competent judges) means more than a moderate increase in their scale of consumption; and vice versa, a judgment that their work is not valued affects them more seriously than would a heavy cut in material consumption. But ordinarily the esteem and the material reward go together. Even where they are immediately in conflict, as when a professional man has chances to do very lucrative work that would lower his professional standing, he is not always prudent, even in money terms, if he takes the bribe. Be that as it may, there must be few so highly energized by these imponderable motives that they are above responding to the incentive of material reward.

The employers of an important executive cannot afford not to equip him with every facility that can economize his time and make his energy as fruitful as possible. This would include a private car and chauffeur, and funds for travel and entertainment, very likely for a really well equipped private library. But these are matters about which it is impossible to say where productive expenditure ends and private consumption begins. They overlap. And it would be absurdly incongruous if, after the executive has been driven to work by his chauffeur, his wife should have to make the beds, vacuum the floors, walk to market, carry supplies home, and personally prepare a meal for distinguished guests, leaving no time or energy to keep in touch with the kinds of things that could enable her to be an adequate and interesting hostess.

It is notorious that high Washington officials find it virtually impossible to live within their salaries. Suppose we conclude that, from this standpoint alone and without regard to differential incentives, an executive of fairly high rank needs at least five times the average income, over and above taxes, and a number of those of the highest rank at least ten times; some perhaps substantially more. If there is a progressive income tax, the income before taxes would have to be correspondingly larger. In other words, purely on an enabling basis and without regard to the stimulus of differential incentives, this calls for a fair number of salaries higher than any government official gets except the President, but still considerably smaller than typical salaries of top executives in large corporations. For present purposes, the precise amount is unimportant.

The top positions in labor unions have grown in time to command salaries that would fit in with the scale suggested, though the general trend of unionism is toward reducing wage differentials. Probably no one can tell with certainty to what extent this equalizing tendency expresses an idea that workers doing similar kinds of work should get equal pay-checks without regard to difference in productivity. A feeling of that sort may enter in, but it is probably a good deal less important than the fear that an extra-productive worker may act as a "pace-setter" for the rest, and they will have to work harder to make the same pay as before. Partly, it goes along with restriction of output to spread work and avoid working one's self out of a job.

The problem of public salaries is interesting. Does government have to pay more because of the competition of high private incomes, or is it able to get its highest officials for less, because most of the persons it would want have private resources which they are willing to use (within limits and for a time) to supplement a government salary that will not support the scale of outside activities required by their positions? Probably it is about as broad as it is long.

One interesting symptom of increasing equality is the partial disappearance of domestic servants. Of course, if there were flat equality of incomes, one person would hardly spend full time in the personal service of another. The change is probably only partly a matter of money, and may be even more due to hours and conditions in domestic service having lagged behind the great improvement that has been made in factory work. The "servant problem" seems to be largely an employer problem. Another kindred symptom is the decline of huge private mansions and great ocean going steam yachts: a combined result of the wage situation and a steeply progressive income tax. I have been told of the Chairman of the Board of one of the country's largest corporations, who is fond of yachting and would like a yacht of a quite modest sort, compared to those that were once commonplace for men in such positions, but he felt he just couldn't quite afford it.

To sum up, we approve of some inequality, but are moving to reduce it. We do not give a superior man his reward mainly in the shape of medals and graded orders, but we have made his money reward in considerable part honorary. He has, in fact, two incomes: the one he receives, which stands as the record of what the economic system rates him as worth, and the one the tax-collector lets him keep. At 1947 rates, if he receives two hundred thousand dollars, he can keep fifty-one thousand dollars of it, and if he earns more, he keeps thirteen and a half cents on the dollar. The rest is just a score on the scoreboard of the economic game he has been playing, showing him to be a very successful player. What does this do to incentives? It probably does not do much, if anything, to reduce the incentive to work hard at the high salaried jobs, but it may interfere substantially with the incentive to risk one's capital in uncertain ventures, where there is always the chance of losing one's investment. It is possible that the tendency to limit inequality at the top has gone about as far as it can usefully go, as long as private capital is relied on for risk-taking investments.

Any inequality at all in the income people are allowed to keep, means that we devote our resources to satisfying less intense wants of the well-to-do, when they could do more good if used to gratify more intense wants of those who are poorer; and this gives concern to some theoretical economists. But under the principle of strategic decisions, if we decide to approve some inequality, we have thereby decided to approve this kind of distortion of the use of resources, because that is what inequality means. Therefore the only thing we can logically regard as a distortion is what results from the wrong kind and degree of inequality. If we approve inequality, we thereby approve its inherent consequences.

10. OPPORTUNITY, SECURITY, JOBS

When we say we want "equality of opportunity," what we mean, perhaps, is as near an approach to equality as is consistent with what we have in the way of inequality of incomes, plus the maintenance of the private family. This could be further defined as a minimum of the material and social conditions of opportunity, sufficient to enable the many who have superior qualities to achieve success more or less proportionate to their capacities and the use they make of them; and to give society the benefit of the great fund of superior quality that arises in unpromising settings. This is a many-sided matter, centering partly in education, partly in access to jobs and partly in social attitudes free from prejudice and unwarranted discrimination. Viewed in this light, it represents a goal toward which we shall have to evolve; some features of it cannot simply be installed overnight by edict. In the matter of education, it includes not only the kind that contributes to personal success, but the kind needed to help develop the responsible attitudes which, as we have seen, are the measure of the amount of freedom we shall be able to preserve.

"Security," too, is many-sided. In general, we have definitely reached the conclusion that a thorough and unmitigated competitive system imposes on the individual a load of insecurity too great for him to bear or to provide against by his own individual efforts. The problem is one of furnishing protection against the really destructive insecurities without wiping out the constructive insecurities that are inseparable from reasonable competitive pressures and individual incentives. Security cannot be made absolute and unconditional. There are still requirements the individual must meet. The livest issue of security at present is security of jobs. This includes a system of industrial jurisprudence that affords protection against arbitrary dismissal, and a system of unemployment insurance. But the most difficult thing to provide is assurance of an adequate total number of jobs.

How many is "adequate"? Lord Beveridge says, "More vacancies than candidates"—which may set an unduly high standard.[1] Others go at it in a different way, reckoning the amount of unemployment due to seasonal causes, terminations and shifts of industry, voluntary labor turnover, discharge for cause and temporary disability. On this basis they may rate employment as adequate when unemployment of all sorts is not more than four or five per cent of the total working force. Our goal of opportunity includes enough job openings so that everyone who meets reasonable requirements can get one—though not necessarily just the job he wants, nor at the moment he wants it. Some say that, to meet the needs of a dynamic economy, there should be enough qualified workers footloose so that new or expanding industries can get workers without having to pull them (or too many of them) away from the working forces of other producers. Others think that there are usually enough workers ready to move from the rural areas (where population expands faster than employment) at any

[1] Full Employment in a Free Society, p. 18.

time when the urban industrial areas have places for them. In any case, if industry needs a reserve corps (not an "industrial reserve army"), the corps needs to be in a tolerable human status, not debilitated or demoralized by long unemployment.

One of the great questions of the time is whether private enterprise can furnish standards of job opportunity that will seem tolerably satisfactory to the bulk of the people. If not, their provisional "strategic decision" to maintain private enterprise is likely to be revised. In the three lectures that follow, we shall be looking at three of the key factors that condition the answer to this problem: spending, prices and wages.

The first requirement is a total volume of spending that will be equal to the income the economy creates when it is working at a satisfactory level, and will enable this level to be maintained and this income to be renewed. This includes spending by individuals, by business and by government; and we have tardily come to understand that it is not automatically self-sustaining, but calls for positive and well-considered action. The next requirement is a level and structure of prices such that an adequate volume of spending may generate a corresponding volume of real production and employment, rather than mere inflation of prices. This in turn calls for a level and structure of wages which will make a proper price-structure possible, wages being the dominant element in costs of production and constituting the third crucial requirement. These are difficult and highly-controversial problems. These lectures cannot hope to resolve all uncertainties about them; but they may serve to clarify issues, and to point the way toward workable policies and—what is more important—toward the underlying attitudes without which sound policies cannot be developed.

THE DIRECT ATTACK: MAINTAINING HIGH-LEVEL DEMAND

1. INTRODUCTION

We have been speaking of objectives. Now we focus on un-employment—and come to questions of ways and means. Such matters are necessarily more technical, dealing with the operation of complicated mechanisms with fallible human working parts. Economists have tardily recognized the importance of the prob-lem, and now for some years the most capable economic minds have been concentrating their main efforts on it. The few cer-tainties they have reached do not tell us just how new devices will work, but on some problems they give us as good a working probability as we can reasonably expect in such cases. They have at least made it hard to say anything both new and true. But there may still be something to be learned from a coördinated survey of the parts of the problem, and an inspection of the principal tools that seem available for dealing with it. We shall probably have occasion to use these tools before many years—always assuming the world avoids the suicidal madness of another war.

Adequate and stable job opportunity rests on two main condi-tions. The first is an adequate and stable volume of demand for goods, expressed in the volume of purchasing, or of potential demand in the shape of readiness and ability to purchase on reason-able terms. That is now our topic. The second is a system that will respond to adequate dollar demand for goods with adequate production and employment, rather than dissipating the effect in inflation of money costs and prices or neutralizing it with various obstructive and restrictive practices. But this necessary division of the subject may be misleading if it is taken to imply that the maintenance of demand is one distinct thing, and the response of the productive system with its mechanism of costs and prices is another separate thing. The pieces react on one another. Total demand is itself affected by the behavior of costs and prices, in ways which economists are still groping to understand.

Most of the demand comes from the automatic action of the cost-price mechanism; and it is only a possible margin of excess or deficiency that needs to be a concern of public policy. In fact, one theory is that all we need to maintain demand is a properly competitive and flexible cost-price mechanism. This theory is an adaptation and extension of the principle that applies to particular products. If your product will not move in the markets, reduce your price until it does move—at some price it is presumably bound to find buyers. Or if you fail to find employment, reduce your wage demands until some employer finds it profitable or practicable to hire you. We shall have a look at this theory in the next two lectures.

In the meantime, we may anticipate the conclusion which will be reached: namely, that a well-behaved system of prices and wages can make it easier to maintain high-level production and employment, and a badly-behaved system can make it harder. Yet even with the best-behaved system that is practically thinkable, this alone cannot be guaranteed to bring about and maintain ample production and employment under all circumstances. A good price-cost structure is necessary, but not sufficient beyond question. At the worst, a badly-behaved structure could make the problem of demand so intractable that it might be impossible, within the limits of the kind of mixed system we call "private enterprise" at present, to bring about results that we would be willing to accept as satisfactory or even tolerable. A proper flow of demand, and a good price-wage structure to respond to it, appear to be jointly necessary.

2. THE PROBLEM OF SPENDING

The problem with which we are dealing gets its shape from a world of buying and selling. This is not the whole of our economic world, but it is the major part of it: the part in which people get what they want by buying it—that is, by first getting money income and then spending it or otherwise disposing of it. They get the income by selling goods or services, and to that end they make things on which other people will spend the income they have gotten, mostly in the same way. When all this is in smooth working order, the (gross cash) income of the maker of each product is composed of the expenditure of the incomes of the makers of the other products, and his expenditures in turn form part of their incomes. Maker's cash income and buyer's expenditure are two sides of the same coin as it passes from hand to hand; they are the two identical entries in a system of double-entry bookkeeping. Neither can increase without an increase in the other.

This identity is the central peg on which the "Keynesian" economics is hung. People have got to make things—that had better not be forgotten, and it will not take care of itself. And they must make things that other people will want to buy, will be able to buy, and will buy. Granted ability and willingness to produce things people want, the active factor in determining how much of this ability and willingness gets employed is the amount of spending. People are not compelled to spend, except perhaps for enough food to keep from going hungry, and other equally urgent necessities. If they suddenly got parsimonious, they could easily cut their total spending twenty per cent for a couple of months, and they would not suffer seriously if that were all that happened.

But after it happened, the makers of the unsold goods would lose their orders and their incomes, and their workers would be

laid off their jobs and would lose their incomes. Then many
people would have a more cogent reason for not spending—because they lacked money to spend. And then total spending, and
income with it, might shrink, not twenty per cent, but forty or
fifty. Thus our system, where spending is voluntary as to time and
amount, is sensitive to disturbances, and can multiply their effect.
For over a century, economists went on the assumption that the
total spending of total income constituted no serious problem, and
would, by and large, take care of itself.[1] It took the depression of
the thirties to convince the majority of them that this is an unsafe
assumption.

Of course, not everything passes through the system of money
purchase and sale. The vegetables some people grow in their back
yards, the cooking and cleaning they do in their own living
quarters, the snow they shovel for themselves—this sort of thing
mounts up to a large total. But for most of us it is subsidiary to
what we get by way of the process of purchase and sale. In earlier
times, many Americans lived in a simpler economy in which they
made most of the things they used. Such was the economy in
which Professor Genung spent his boyhood, so sympathetically
pictured by John Erskine.[2] Then all one needed for employment
was one's wants and one's hands, the materials that were available
and the inherited knowledge, plus Yankee wit and gumption,
which went into the fashioning of the products. If one's time were
not needed for one thing, there were always other things one
wanted. If someone else would pay for some of the things one
produced, one might be richer; but one never need be idle because the outside purchaser failed to appear.

Some of the work constituted investment for future consumption or future return. When the family made a season's supply of
soap, or smoked a winter's provision of meat, they were "accumulating inventory," but no one's livelihood was endangered by over-

---

[1] I have dealt with this briefly in Alternative to Serfdom, esp. pp. 93–95.
[2] See The Memory of Certain Persons, pp. 125–6.

accumulation. When they made a table or shingled the barn, they were acquiring durable capital goods. But there was no menace of idleness when the barn was shingled or the table finished. When idle moments came, it was because their own wants were momentarily provided for, not because someone else, consulting his own convenience as to when he wanted products, had left them without employment, and therefore without both goods and income. When you shingle your own barn, you do it when you have time for it; when you shingle someone else's, you do it when and if he wants it done. And when you are a carpenter and not a farmer, that contingency becomes potentially serious.

People buy food fairly regularly, if they have the money. Buying clothes is a bit seasonal, but still fairly dependable from season to season—clothes wear out at a fairly steady rate and have to be replaced. Automobiles and expensive household appliances are bought when people have money, or when they feel confident enough about future money to be willing to sign an instalment contract. Then if that confidence weakens, there may come a time when purchasers are using their income to pay off outstanding contracts, and few new ones are being signed; and then something will happen to the sales of automobiles and household appliances. Commercial inventories are notoriously prone to swell or shrink as business gains or loses confidence. When they swell, something is added to the demand of the ultimate purchaser; when they shrink, something is subtracted. And long-lived construction, for housing or industry, faces a demand that is liable to the widest fluctuations. Spending for capital outlays, especially in a system of private business enterprise, can be violently spasmodic, speeding up or slowing down. The fluctuations of spending concentrate on durable goods, and especially durable goods bought or constructed for business use. But if there is any question of the long-run adequacy of spending, spending for consumption and investment become equally important.

In a simpler kind of money economy, people cannot make

capital outlays until they have saved up the money, out of their previous income, or until they have found someone else who has saved money, and is willing to lend it to them. Under those conditions, expansions would be slower than they actually are, but steadier. At present, the advocates of one hundred per cent reserve banking are, in effect, trying to bring us back nearer to that simple state in which income has to be saved before it can be spent for capital outlays. But with the kind of expansible credit system we have, people can borrow funds and spend them without waiting for anyone to save them first. So the expansion of spending is cut loose from the limits of prior income, and the timing of spending is free to follow the desire of the spender, (if he has credit), and to disregard the requirements of stability. The system can expand faster, and more spasmodically; and when it goes into reverse, it may contract faster.

All this lends explosive force to the simple freedom of the purchaser to control his own spending. He can buy what he wants —well and good. But he can also buy when he wants, and stop buying for any reason or no reason. In a cash economy, the unstabilizing effects of this freedom might be limited; but when it is equipped with the resources of an elastic credit system, it gains the power to blow inflationary balloons and prick them. The freedom to spend becomes a distinctly unsafe one, because when A stops spending, B stops receiving income, then B stops employing C, and C curtails his spending; and the spiral goes on until something stops it or turns it in the other direction.

Going back to the simple self-sufficing economy—if a person can get access to things to work with, or on, the only thing that will stop him from working is to reach a point at which more goods are not worth the trouble of doing more work to get them. And that, of course, is not what is meant by "unemployment" of the involuntary sort. If a modern economy reaches a corresponding point, why does it not act in the same way? Instead, workers are laid off or put on part time when they still want more goods, and

would gladly work longer to get them. Even at normal employment, many individual workers would work overtime if they had
the option, even without premium pay. Historically, the system
of paying time-and-a-half for overtime beyond forty hours was
adopted, not as an incentive to the worker to work longer, but
as a deterrent to the employer, penalizing him for having his
employes work more than forty hours. The object was to spread
an amount of work that was less than the workers would willingly
do, if it were left to them to say whether more goods were worth
the trouble of doing more work to get them.

One way of putting the reason is to say that some people, when
they have reached the point where they do not want more present
goods, still want more income, and will work for it, turning out
goods that other people may or may not want. People want income
which they do not want to spend—not now—they want deferred
claims to goods. But there are only two ways in which the economy
as a whole can get deferred claims. One is to make goods that are
not currently wanted and store them. But there are few goods
that are sure enough of holding their value to make this process
safe or attractive. The second way is to make capital equipment to
produce more goods, or to render future services—this includes
building residential housing to sell or rent. In either case, the
economy is making physical capital, in the form of inventory or
equipment. And the amount of deferred claims the economy as a
whole can get is limited to the amount of such capital it is willing
to make.

All of which may be just another way of putting the Keynesian
theorem that, for the economy as a whole, savings cannot exceed
investment. When some try to save more than others are willing
to invest, the income they started with is not all spent in ways that
generate more income. The part that stands idle is lost to the
economy as a whole. Hence the income of the society shrinks to
the amount that its members are willing to take in the form of
goods currently produced; and people who wanted more income

cannot get it, because others are not spending theirs for currently-produced goods. It comes down to the relatively simple proposition with which we started, that in the money economy, every man's income is made up of other people's spendings, and the spendings are the active factor governing the amount of the income. The indicated need is therefore to keep spending stable and adequate, in a system in which individuals are not compelled to spend any particular amount at any particular time.

If people's spending equals the income of the immediate past, the past income will be renewed in unchanged amount. If they spend less, money income shrinks; if they spend more, money income increases. And, if this line of analysis means what it seems to mean, then it is the only way in which money income can increase. The implications of that are far-reaching and disturbing. To put it in a challenging way (which is partly misleading) individuals get richer by spending less than their incomes; society gets richer by spending more. Naturally, that is an oversimplification. "Getting richer" does not mean the same thing in the two cases. For the individual, it means accumulating deferred claims. For society, it means increasing its current income. An individual can also get rich by increasing his current income—but only if someone is spending more for the goods or services he has for sale.

3. KINDS OF SPENDING

Anything like a full tracing of the flow of spendings and receipts becomes bafflingly complicated, and they can be classified in different ways, for different purposes.[1] The main divisions are: private consumers' spending (often loosely spoken of as "consumption"); private capital outlays, gross and net; and government spending, for currently-used goods and services, and for durable assets. As to whether these last should be classified as consumption or capital outlays, the line may be drawn in three different places, each perhaps appropriate to a different purpose.

[1] For an introduction to this complexity, by way of simplified models, see Carl Shoup, "Principles of National Income Analysis."

For some purposes, mere durability is the key; and for these purposes all durables are alike, including those bought by private consumers. Such things are bought at one time, and render more or less continuous service thereafter, with the result that the spending that calls forth their production can be intermittent, speeding up or slowing down, without an equal change in the flow of services the durables render. People can stop building houses without having to stop living in the houses already built. For another purpose, the important thing is whether or not these durable goods are fairly directly used to assist the processes of private production, like a truck highway or a laboratory for public research for industrial uses. For still another purpose the important thing is how the expenditures for these durables are financed, and here the important distinction is between outlays that are "self-liquidating" and "non-self-liquidating": that is, whether they are financed out of payments for their direct services or out of the general public funds, most of which have to be raised by taxes.

Foreign trade raises another set of problems. Some of the spending for American products is done by foreigners, and some American spending goes for foreign products. So the spending that energizes American production and employment includes a balance, plus or minus, representing the difference between these two items. For this purpose, it makes no difference whether the foreigners who buy American steel are exporting it or using it to build a factory in this country—import of "capital" or export of goods have the same effect on the balance of payments. But from the standpoint of the satiation of American needs, it may make a good deal of difference. If our government furnishes the funds for our own exports, as it is doing now on a huge scale, the direct effect on spending here is the same as if it spent the money here for bomber planes or post offices; but if it is spent for food, the effect on our available supplies of foodstuffs is different.

In general, the principal item in the international balance consists of exports and imports of commodities. When this country has an excess of exports, as it has had since World War I, this means that our domestic spending is supplemented by foreign spending (except as we may ourselves furnish the funds in ways that reduce our domestic spending, in which case the export balance is not a clear addition). This gives our economy a stimulus, so long as we are in a condition in which the limiting factor is demand for our products, not our own power to produce them. If it goes beyond that, it may be an overstimulus, leading to inflation. In either case it is a stimulus of a sort that, by its nature, cannot last forever.

4. WHERE SPENDING COMES FROM—IS PUBLIC SPENDING PARASITIC?

Where does spending come from? This can be looked at in two ways, which should be complementary. Spending comes out of the existing supply of currency and bank deposits and the rate at which people are willing to pass them on to others, plus or minus any net increase or decrease in the total amount of such means of payment. (That is not a mathematical formula, but indicates the materials out of which one might be made.) But what makes people willing to part with the means of payment they hold? Chiefly the fact that they are currently receiving income to replace their spendings (consumer outlays) or they hope, by making business or capital outlays now, to receive income later. Thus we get the alternative formula: spending comes out of current income; or today's spending comes out of yesterday's income, plus any net discrepancy resulting from dissaving or individual investment in excess of yesterday's saving, or minus any discrepancy of the opposite sort.

Most income, and most spendings, come out of business operations. A business may make disbursements to other businesses, chiefly for materials, or it may disburse funds to individuals, workers and security-holders, and the funds are then spent by them. But one large stream is diverted into taxes, which take parts of the income both before and after the business disburses it as income to individuals. Taxes, of course, are not an independent source of income.[1] Another large diverted stream consists of savings that are borrowed and spent. But, as we have seen, with an elastic credit system, borrowing and spending is not tied to prior saving; it can be greater or less; and this discrepancy becomes a further important item, plus or minus, in the generation of spending.

But if personal incomes, taxes and most borrowings all come out of incomes derived from business operations, then it would seem that we have almost said that all spending comes, directly or indirectly, from business income. This has an element of truth, but needs so many qualifications that it is, on the whole, more misleading than enlightening. It serves chiefly, perhaps, to explain how people who are business-minded look at publicly-financed activities as parasitic burdens on the back of the productive activities of private business, which are conceived as the only economically self-supporting and productive ones. This is a half-truth; and as with many half-truths, the population is largely divided into those who see it as the whole truth and those who see it as no truth at all. Neither view is correct.

In the first place, any self-liquidating public activities would have to be classed under "business." In the second place, as to services supported out of taxes instead of prices paid for the services rendered, while the taxpayer feels differently about paying a tax and about paying a price for something specific he has received, the effect on his income is the same—something is subtracted to pay the costs of the service. The important question is whether the service is worth the cost; and the answer would seem to be that some are and some are not, under both private and public systems.

5. WHAT CONTROLS THE AMOUNT OF SPENDING?

What, then, does the amount of spending depend on? It depends largely on the income of the immediate past, and on

---

[1] A successful capital levy might be an exception, but there is doubt whether such a levy can be laid which will not actually be paid out of income.

how that income is distributed. It depends on how strong is the pressure of unsatisfied wants and needs in that complex thing we call the "standard of living." It depends on the disposition to save, and all the things that may strengthen or weaken it, including social provision for future needs, which may supplement individual saving, and may or may not partially replace it. Finally, it depends on the disposition to adventure one's assets (or other people's assets) for a profit, and at a risk of loss. Does it also depend on the volume of money and money equivalents in form available to make money payments? Perhaps, to some extent, but it is difficult to say how far this acts as an independent cause. Within wide limits, it seems to be the other way around; the supply of banking means of payment accommodates itself to the volume of spending. It has great unused powers of expansion; and it has demonstrated a capacity to stand partly idle (reducing its "velocity of circulation") if the volume of spending is smaller than the existing means of payment can easily handle.

The first form of the Full Employment Act directed the use of stimulative measures when needed to increase employment, public spending being the one type of measure clearly indicated. The executive, however, would actually have to seek further Congressional action to carry out this directive. In its final form, the act recognizes more of the realities of the problem, including the variety of possible policies, the margins of uncertainty as to their precise effect, and the need of further Congressional sanction for any really substantial action. This act was stimulated by the war, which tended toward an oversimplified view of the peacetime problem. People said: "The war proved we can have full employment, if we will do the necessary things"; and the crucial necessary thing appeared to be enormous public spending, partly financed by borrowed money. This makes it pertinent to ask: "What did the war really prove—what lessons, that is, that are applicable to peace time?"

6. WHAT DID THE WAR PROVE?

Actually, the war experience included a combination of factors, most of which could not be reproduced in peace time. The main ones were the following.

(1) It included deficit spending on a scale that would, in normal peace time, have alarmed business to the point of paralyzing voluntary private capital outlays.

(2) Business fear of deficits was temporarily submerged by the emergency.

(3) Government was willing to give private capital extraordinary amortization privileges, to minimize the uncertainties of investment for war production, and was willing to put up the bulk of the capital itself.

(4) There was a tremendous increase in the total real need for things. We were making tanks and B-17's because we had to have them, not for the sake of making work. And we needed them, not instead of ordinary peace-time goods, but in addition. Vitally needed as they were, they were no substitute for the goods that met normal civilian needs. From this standpoint they had the quality of uselessness in ideal degree; they did not displace civilian demand, but mainly competed with it for supply of labor and materials.

(5) Patriotic incentives were aroused enough to be a substantial factor, however much they were entangled with ordinary business motives. For that reason many mechanisms worked better than the same mechanisms would work in normal peace time.

The result was more-than-full employment, plus inflation. The inflation was kept within moderate bounds by direct controls, despite lenient treatment of large areas of the price structure, including farm prices, prices of special war-*matériel*, and wages. These direct controls were barely tolerated, on the understanding that they were strictly temporary emergency measures; and even during the "shooting war" they led a precarious existence, needing to be constantly on guard against attacks aiming to emasculate them. This temporary and grudging tolerance for controls of prices and wages is the sixth major factor special to the war experience and accounting for the results.

7. HOW THE PRESENT SITUATION DIFFERS FROM THAT OF THE WAR [1]

Since the end of fighting we have had high employment and renewed inflation, with no direct controls to keep it in check since 1946. The government is at present paying out less than it takes in, and those who have been spending in excess of yesterday's income would seem to be private individuals or businesses. Consumer expenditures appear to have been above their normal percentage of the disposable incomes of individuals (income after taxes). There may be several reasons for this. Many consumers have war savings, some of which they expected to spend when postwar goods were available, and which may enable them to spend closer to their incomes than would ordinarily be safe. As a result of the steeply progressive personal income tax, it seems certain that disposable income is more evenly distributed than before the war, and this would naturally tend to cause a slightly greater percentage of it to be spent for consumption. Thirdly, many consumers have had a wartime taste of more liberal consumption than they had been accustomed to, and their tastes may have been permanently enlarged.

In addition to consumption, there is a concentrated demand for housing and capital outlays generally, to make up for years of depression and war, when such expenditures were either abnormally small, or were diverted away from the things that would satisfy peace-time needs. This "backlog" of unsatisfied demand is not permanent, but it is so large that it may last through the period that would normally be marked by several short business cycles. The demand for European aid is another temporary one;

[1] The conditions described are those of the winter of 1947–8.

but the changed channels of European trade may bring about an enduring increase in the demand for American agricultural products, to make up for reduced supplies which western Europe is receiving from eastern Europe, as the satellite countries are induced to do more of their trading with Russia and less with western Europe. As a combined result of all these things, we have had excessive spending, giving us about as much inflation since the war ended as we had while it was going on—indeed more in absolute terms.

For the present we may postpone the question of inflation and go on to the question of what will happen when this temporary condition of high spending ends, and when spending may threaten to become too small. If that happens, we shall be facing the double problem of stabilizing spending when it develops insta-bility, and possibly counteracting a long-run tendency for the total amount to decline.

8. WHAT IS THE IDEAL ADJUSTMENT?

The conditions necessary to stability are indicated by the things that make for instability. The most unstable sector of spending consists of capital outlays and spending for other highly durable goods. Other kinds of spending probably fluctuate for the most part because people's incomes have fluctuated; and the incomes fluctuated primarily because of fluctuating spending in the sector of durable goods and capital outlays. This is commonplace by now, but some of the consequences may not be so generally appreciated. It means that the highest levels of consumption we ever reach are reached when we are, to put it roughly, crowding two years' capital outlays into one year, and spending on durables and capital out-lays at a rate which cannot be maintained. So the first requisite is to stabilize this sensitive sector of spending.

But if it is stabilized at an average rate, then consumer-outlays also will be less than they are at peaks of business activity, and total spending will fall short of what is required for full employment. And capital outlays, at least of the business sort, cannot be arbitrarily increased, because they have to be kept within the limits of the amounts on which business can collect a return in the prices people voluntarily pay for the products. The conclusion is inescapable; a stable high level of income depends, among other things, on combining stabilized capital outlays with increased consumer-spending, so that total demand will still be high enough, without the stimulus of a rate of capital outlays that is too high to be maintained. These two conditions are complementary; but the consumer side is generally forgotten while attention is centered on the primary offender—unstable capital outlays.

The ideal balance may include shorter hours of work, but only insofar as the resulting leisure is worth more than the added product that might be gotten from maintaining former hours of work. Hours are sometimes shortened more than they would be for the sake of the added leisure, in order to share work when there is not enough work to go around. This, of course, is not an ideal balance, in principle, but represents a sharing of involuntary unemployment. Perhaps the chief saving factor in this situation is the consideration that workers, left to themselves and driven by family responsibilities, would often choose to work longer than is good for their health, to increase their immediate earnings. In view of this, perhaps a little pressure of the work-sharing sort may bring about a better-balanced working week than completely free individual choice would do, when personal health is taken into account.

Finally, if total spending is to be adequate in the long run, there needs to be a balance between the savings people want to make, when they are as well off as high-level employment will make them, and the capital outlays and other items of similar effect, which take the savings and put them to work, or at least cause an equivalent amount of spending. Perhaps this is merely the inverse side of the balance between consumption and capital outlays, with which we started. It describes a condition that cannot be trusted to come about automatically, and if not, there may be chronic underemployment. Part of a high standard of living is adequate provision for the future, and this normally means saving. Where the standard of future provision is high, it is conceivable that people will want to save more of their income than industry will find remunerative use for—remunerative enough to enable it to pay the kind of return the savers expect on their savings. And in that case, some other kind of adjustment is needed, if an ample national income is to be spent, and thereby renew itself. So the problem of policy is to find how to bring things as near as possible to the ideal adjustment, or how to work out the best practicable substitute, when the ideal adjustment does not come of its own accord.

9. FLUCTUATIONS: THEIR CUMULATIVE EFFECTS

It used to be thought that the problem would be solved if we could stabilize fluctuations, so we may look at that aspect first. One reason why spending fluctuates so much is because any general change in the amount of spending involves a change in incomes, and this causes a further change in spending, and so on indefinitely. These cumulative effects create our greatest difficulties; but if we can learn how to influence the total amount of spending in the direction we want, the cumulative effects will work with us instead of against us. Hence this difficulty is also an opportunity.

So far as consumer spending is concerned, we have enough evidence about its responses to changes in income to be able to make useful surmises, at least, as to the size of the derived effects of any initial change. If the initiating factor is an increase in spending, this increases income, and part of the increase is spent, creating further income, and so on in a theoretically endless but decreasing series, with a finite sum. If the initial addition to spending is not repeated, the normal after-effect would soon dwindle to zero. But if the additional spending is continued, the aftereffects mount up, at a decreasing rate. On simplified assumptions, it would approach limits which have sometimes been computed with misleading precision. Under favorable conditions, an initial increase might be multiplied by three or more, most of the derived effect coming about within two years or less. This effect goes by the name of the "multiplier."

So far, we have been considering only the response of consumer spending of the ordinary sort. But when one takes into account the effects on capital outlays and on consumer products which are so highly durable that they behave like capital outlays, these effects appear to be highly variable, in a way that depends on time and circumstance, with the result that the precise conception of a "multiplier" becomes more misleading than helpful. Under favorable conditions and for a limited time, an original increase of three dollars might lead to a two-dollar increase in consumer spending, plus two dollars in capital outlays, so three dollars would breed four, and the four would breed five-and-one-third, and so on at an increasing rate rather than a diminishing one. Then the effects might be infinite and not finite, if this reaction could go on to infinity. The trouble is that it cannot; the wave of capital outlays, or of stocking up with long-lived durable goods, will exhaust itself in time, and then the effect will be reversed. Spending will shrink, and the shrinkage will cumulate as the expansion did. And this is what we want to prevent. Or if an increase in consumer spending is brought about by policies that discourage capital outlays, then the derived effects may be a minus quantity instead of a plus, and income may shrink without any preliminary expansion.

The problem is to increase spending, when needed, in ways that will avoid this minus effect; and if the effect is plus, to handle it in such a way that it may taper off into a stable level of high activity, rather than leading to a revulsion. And that is far from simple or easy.

10. STABILIZING FLUCTUATIONS

The chief generating source of fluctuations is in capital outlays, while the most predictable (and hence potentially controllable) derived fluctuations are in consumer spending. Capital outlays constitute much the smaller total amount, but they fluctuate much more violently, so that the total fluctuation, in an ordinary business cycle, is roughly similar in amount. And policies of stabilization may work on either sector. If nothing will do short of complete stabilization, one must take hold of the originating causes and stabilize capital outlays. But important mitigating effects can be accomplished by reducing the derived fluctuations in consumer spending; and within limits this is the sector of private spending that is easier to influence, and responds more dependably. Another way of classifying policies is into those that have a "built-in" or automatic stabilizing effect, and those that require positive action—a decision or an order—to bring them into play.

"Built-in" stabilization applies mainly to the derived fluctuations of consumer spending, and is limited to mitigating their amount. We have two main kinds of built-in mitigators: social security provisions for unemployment compensation, and a progressive income tax. The effect of unemployment compensation is obvious; it collects funds when people are working and earning wages, and pays them out when people are out of work, thus mitigating their loss of income, and tending to sustain their spending power. It is not practicable to cancel the entire loss of income, for obvious reasons. If people could receive as much for doing nothing as for working full time, there would be too much temptation to malingering. The benefits are a fraction of full pay, there is usually a waiting period, qualifications for elegibility, and a limit of time beyond which benefits cease. All these limitations reduce the total compensation paid, so that in the past it has offset about ten per cent of the shrinkage in the workers' incomes resulting from a recession of business. Professor S. H. Slichter has estimated that, with what has been learned from our experience to date, it is now practicable to liberalize the provisions, and so raise the ten per cent to twenty-five per cent or even thirty per cent.[1]

This would be a substantial mitigation of the shrinkage in the workers' buying power, but only that. And it would raise the cost of the benefits so much that methods of financing would need to be reconsidered, or else the tax that is laid on the act of employing labor, to support the unemployment benefits, might become too substantial a handicap to employment, and so defeat its own end. As Lord Beveridge has pointed out, such liberal benefits might become a prohibitive burden unless unemployment is kept low, with the help of other measures.[2]

In this connection, the proposal for a guaranteed annual wage might be regarded as similar in general effect, only going much farther in stabilizing the buying power of the workers who receive the guarantee. It would face the same kind of difficulties of financing, in more extreme form. If industry has already reduced depression-unemployment to small proportions, a guaranteed wage could act cumulatively, reducing cyclical declines still further. But as things are, one is forced to the conclusion that the burden would stifle employment in industries faced with unstable demand, for reasons beyond their individual control—and there are many such. We shall return to this question in connection with collective bargaining and the wage structure.

Work relief is another way of sustaining workers' buying power, but it faces its own difficulties, as the experience of the great depression showed. The weekly earnings it affords should naturally be more than outright unemployment benefits, but less than earnings in normal private employment, so that the workers may have an incentive to take regular jobs, and put an end to the inefficient use of manpower which work relief represents. But if unemployment benefits are raised, it will be even harder than in the past to

[1] Cf. Public Policies and Postwar Employment, in Financing American Prosperity, p. 276.

[2] Social Insurance and Allied Services (the "Beveridge Report") p. 163.

fix wage scales and working schedules that will meet these requirements.

Another way of sustaining private consumer buying consists of subsidizing private consumption of surplus goods, as was done under the food-stamp plan. This seems to be chiefly of use in connection with an agricultural program, and its effect in sustaining demand seems to be chiefly of benefit to farmers. It needs to be handled in such a way as to insure that the subsidized demand is added to the buying that would otherwise be done, and not substituted for it; and this means, in turn, that it is confined to people who are undernourished because of low buying power. It might have some slight effect in stabilizing demand, but its usefulness seems to be narrowly limited.

More positive effects in stabilizing demand seem to hinge on stabilization of capital outlays, including for this purpose residential construction. Here one method which was prominent in the thinking on the problem, twenty years and more ago, was to restrain the peaks of business booms, on the theory that the cause of a depression is the boom that precedes it. This is a half-truth, and contains its own dangers. The first effect of a policy of this sort would at best be merely to strike an average between boom and depression thus stabilizing a medium amount of underemployment. Then real success depends on the existence of natural forces that would automatically absorb this underemployment when it become chronic, and raise the average up to a satisfactory level. And that is something about which present day economists are increasingly doubtful. Failing that, the policy would need to be combined with other measures of a long-run sustaining sort, directed to absorbing any chronic underemployment that might appear. The policy of whittling down peaks may have its place, but is only part of a total policy.

It has its positive dangers, too. Its most appropriate instrument is the credit system. But no credit authority would apply restrictive measures until it was sure that expansion had gone too far, and then it would be likely to begin cautiously and tentatively, with measures intended mainly as warnings. If serious restrictions turned out to be needed, it would be remarkable if they did not come too late for the best results, and at a time when they would be much more likely to precipitate an impending depression than to avoid it by checking a boom before it went to unhealthy lengths. Success would require a close approach to perfection in a delicate job of timing, gauging the amount of restriction and selecting the points at which to apply it. The simplest and most impersonal form of restriction—raising the rate of interest—cannot be freely used under postwar conditions, because it would reduce the value of government bonds, and undermine the technical solvency of banks and other financial institutions which have a large part of their assets invested in these bonds.

Ideally, a program of restricting booms might keep the expansion of capital outlays down to a rate that could be sustained indefinitely. Practically, this could never be measured with any certainty; there would be a margin of doubt, and expansion would be given the benefit of it. But it would be well worth trying to gauge the maximum and minimum limits within which normal sustained capital outlays must fall. We would not get rid of uncertainty, but we might learn something useful. The credit mechanism is more suited to restricting activity than to expanding it. It can make money "easy," but that will not insure its being taken and used, if business does not see openings in which the prospect of return is worth the risk of the principal. Or as the bankers say: "You can't push on a string."

This raises the question whether business can be afforded more positive incentives to make capital outlays in dull times, and so make them less dull. One prescription is to let the prices of capital goods go down to bargain levels. As an effective stabilizer, this faces numerous difficulties, which we shall examine in the next lecture. By way of a different kind of incentive, it has been suggested that government might give financial inducements in the shape of tax rebates, or even subsidies, in return for agreements to purchase durable goods or carry out capital outlays, or to maintain stable inventories, or to hold capital projects in readiness, to be carried out at such time as a government agency might indicate that they were needed.[1] If government were willing to take the initiative and offer the financial inducements, this might obviate the need for the private interests getting together and accepting heavy reductions in their usual compensation. Along with this goes the danger of supporting prices and wages that have been pegged too high. By one device or another, there are possibilities in the general direction of stabilization of demand in the field of capital outlays, once people accept the idea that for such stabilization it is worth taking considerable trouble and doing a number of unconventional things.

Obviously, if the government is willing to go to all this trouble, it would also be willing to manage its own capital outlays so that they would serve a stabilization program. Three different grades of objective have been suggested.

(1) Stabilize the volume of public works. This, of course, would leave private construction to fluctuate; but it would be an important mitigation. It would seem that the federal government must either induce state and local governments to cooperate in an over-all stabilization program, or else time its own public works so as to counteract the fluctuations of state and local outlays. Neither of these is easy.

(2) Stabilize the construction industry. This requires government as a whole to time its public works so that they will fluctuate counter to the fluctuations of private construction. This is a large order. It would surely need the active cooperation of state and local governments, and it might call for more counter-cyclical

[1] Cf. Morris A. Copeland, Business Stabilization by Agreement, Amer. Econ. Rev., June, 1944, pp. 328–339.

fluctuation than could be brought about merely by shifting the timing of the work that would in any case be done over a ten-year period. It might require some additional projects.

(3) Make construction fluctuate counter cyclically, to an extent sufficient to counteract the fluctuations in other capital outlays, and so stabilize capital outlays as a whole. If this could be done, cyclical fluctuations in business as a whole would be a thing of the past. But business is not a whole, and in the construction industry, counter cyclical fluctuations would be about as uncomfortable as cyclical ones; and the industry would not appreciate having them deliberately imposed upon it. If this meant temporarily turning mechanics or clerks into road-workers or bricklayers, it would probably take the most extreme national emergency to jolt people that far out of their accustomed occupations.

Stabilizing the construction industry by timing of public works presents many difficulties. It is not easy to induce state and local governments to cooperate closely enough so that their timing will be really helpful. It is hard to find a sufficient number of projects that are worth doing (meaning they are needed) but can be anticipated or postponed without seriously impairing their value. Big projects are slow in reaching the stage at which they employ their full force, and once they are started, it is wasteful to tamper with their normal speed of prosecution. In the light of these difficulties, a fair guess seems to be that the timing of normal public works alone is not likely to succeed in stabilizing the construction industry. If private construction were made less unstable by the kinds of policies and incentives already sketched, public works might be able to do the rest of the job. Otherwise, stabilization of the construction industry would probably require an expansion of the present field of public works. This might mean increased government participation in such things as slum clearance projects, or it might mean the taking over of a limited number of private industries which involve large capital outlays. Thus we should move in the direction of a "mixed system" of public and private industry.

If private industry became convinced that this is the alternative, the realization might make it more willing to participate in publicly stimulated regularization of private capital outlays.

So much for flexible capital outlays, public and private. Another potential stabilizer consists of flexible public revenues, which would mitigate the fluctuations of spendable income by collecting a smaller percentage when income shrinks, and a larger one when it expands. A progressive income tax does this automatically, to a limited extent; but from the standpoint of sustaining spending, it may not do it in the most useful way. If all incomes shrink ten per cent, a person with an initial taxable income of one hundred thousand dollars gets a tax reduction that cancels between eighty-two per cent and eighty-three per cent of the shrinkage; his income after taxes is reduced about four and seven-tenths per cent, instead of ten per cent. A person with a taxable income of two thousand dollars and an exemption of one thousand dollars gets a tax reduction cancelling nineteen per cent of his shrinkage in income; his income after taxes is reduced eight and ninety-five hundredths per cent instead of ten per cent.[1] In other words, the largest relief goes where it will do the least to sustain consumer spending.

For more substantial results, tax rates would have to be changed; and the only workable way of doing this, as a business cycle stabilizer, would be for Congress to establish a formula calling for specified changes in rates (including probably the base-rate and exemptions) when specified statistical indexes reach specified points, or show specified amounts of increase or decrease. This would provide for prompt action (which would be impossible if Congress had to debate each change of rates) without leaving the setting of tax rates at the discretion of the executive. The same sort of thing could be done with social security taxes. In each case, the aim would presumably be to set a schedule of rates that would provide the desired amount of revenue at normal average

[1] These calculations were made at 1947 rates; with altered rates, the same principle applies and the same general kind of result follows.

rates of business activity over, let us say, a ten-year period. There would be deficits in depressed times, and surpluses during booms. For that matter, this would be true if the rates remained fixed; but with flexible rates, both deficits and surpluses would be larger. A more radical plan would be to balance the budget in good times, and allow deficits in depressions.

Such financing is unorthodox, but logical. Perhaps the greatest obstacle to getting it adopted is the fact that it would take a spell of hard times to convince Congress of the need for anything so unconventional; but hard times would not be a suitable time to initiate such a method of taxing. This is a real difficulty, but it ought not to be fatal—we ought to be able to deal with these questions at a slightly higher level than the settler who couldn't mend his leaky roof when it was raining, and when it wasn't raining, the roof didn't leak.

11. SUSTAINING THE AVERAGE LEVEL OF DEMAND

For the present, we are embarrassed with too much demand, not too little; and with problems of inflation, not unemployment. This state of things bids fair to continue as long as "Marshall plan" aid is flowing in a full current. But this will not last forever; within the next five years there is a considerable likelihood that we shall find demand becoming too small, not too large. This may last longer than the ordinary cyclical depression (following the un-usually-long postwar boom) and we may confront the question whether the country is in a chronic condition in which it will not spend all the income it is willing and able to produce. Are we unwilling to consider that possibility in advance, and unwilling to get ready to do something about it? That would put us in a class with the settler who would not mend his roof.

The problem is more difficult than that of mere stabilization. Stabilization calls mainly for a shift in the timing of the receipt of income by individuals, and in outlays for capital and durables, from times of boom to those of depression; raising the average level calls for an increase in the total of spending. We have looked briefly at the main factors controlling the different kinds of spending; and this ought to give clues as to ways and means of influencing the amount. The trouble is, it gives too many clues, and some of the policies based on them would conflict. It is not hard to devise measures that will increase one kind of spending, but it is not so easy to be sure what effect they will have on other kinds.

Public spending may encroach on private spending in two ways: the products or services may compete with privately-produced products or services and displace them, or the funds to pay for the public products or services may be subtracted from the funds that would otherwise be spent for other private services or goods. On the other hand, one kind of spending may generate other kinds, as improved transportation may open up an area for industrial or suburban development. Most spending has a mixture of these plus and minus effects, and either the plus or the minus may be the larger. The problem is to select policies that will have the largest possible net balance of positive effect. Initially, they should add more spending than they displace, and, so far as possible, the aftereffects should be such as to generate further activities rather than merely leaving fewer wants unsatisfied. All this is possible, but by no means easy.

The most obvious and simple method, if private spending is insufficient, is for government to fill the gap by spending more. But if it raises the funds by increased taxation, it cuts into the spending of the taxpayers, first by reducing their "disposable income," out of which their current spending is financed, and further by impairing their incentive to make capital outlays. So far as the first is concerned, the reduction of private spending is likely to be somewhat less than the increase in government spending—a dollar added to taxes may reduce consumer spending by something like eighty cents, leaving a net margin of twenty cents increase in the total as the direct and immediate effect. The effect on capital outlays is more conjectural; increased demand for goods and services would tend to cause increased capital outlays, unless the accompanying tax structure lays discouraging burdens on the potential investor, or makes him distrustful of the soundness of the economy. In that case, the over-all net effect might be a minus quantity.

Granting that the thing could be done in ways that would increase total spending, there is still a serious objection to face. Government is presumably spending as much as the community thinks it worth-while to allocate to the kinds of services government renders. In which case, increased spending would mean diverting resources to products of inferior value, by the community's existing standards: things that do not compete with private spending simply because private individuals do not want the products enough to be willing to pay their costs. But there is no need to advocate spending for useless things merely to increase spending for its own sake, though Lord Keynes once made some unguarded remarks about the usefulness of building pyramids, if nothing better offered.

Better things do offer. Alvin H. Hansen has listed four major categories in which increased public spending would be eminently useful: health, nutrition, education and housing.[1] In some parts of this list there are problems of avoiding conflict between public and private spending, but the need of an increased total is hard to deny. No pyramids are called for. There can be little question that increased spending in these categories is more useful than spending on the inanities of rhymed commercials, the worse-than-inanities of the perfume and patent medicine advertisements, and other forms of private spending that could be named. Such a shift would make the community's spending more productive, not less.[2]

[1] See A. H. Hansen, Economic Policy and Full Employment, p. 167.

[2] At this point I seem to hear a flood of objections; chiefly that I am expressing an ethical or political judgment, not an economic one. In anticipatory rebuttal, I deny that ethical or political judgments and economic ones are mutually exclusive; they are simply different methods of balancing values and costs, under circumstances which lead to different weighting of the considerations involved. Each has, in practice, its strong and weak points, as com-

The main element of truth in the theory that public spending is a parasitic burden relates, not to the social productiveness of the services government renders, but to the mechanism for financing payment for them. There appear to be limits on the extent to which government can divert money incomes from what the owners want to do with it to things the government thinks it should be spent for. One eminent economist has estimated that, over a long period, not more than a quarter of the national income can be taken in taxes without serious consequences; another has suggested two thirds as the maximum rate of income tax that can be laid on the top brackets without severely interfering with the business incentives to productive activity. Our present top-bracket rates are well above this.

Perhaps the basic reason for limits on taxation is that when a person buys something and pays for it, he feels that he is getting a quid pro quo, so that his real income is not reduced by the spending; he is merely realizing on it, and deciding in what form he wants to take it. But when the same person pays a tax, he does not feel that he is getting any specific quid pro quo, and he does feel that the tax is a subtraction from his income, not a mere question of realizing on it in the form of public services rather than private goods. If he is a top-bracket income tax payer, he is quite correct in this feeling. The tax does make him poorer; and he is paying far more than the cost of any specific services he receives.

When taxes reach their limit, or what people feel is their limit, there is still borrowing. In fact, some of the newer theorists would say: why wait till taxes reach their limit? We need taxes now, because we are spending too much—we have inflation—but when the time comes when we are spending too little, why not simply increase public spending without increasing taxes? Then every dollar the government spent would be a clear net increase, instead

---

pared to the others. In contending that the views I have expressed represent the prevailing actual standard of values, I am appealing to what I am convinced is the inevitable judgment of any informed and open-minded citizen who can be brought to look at the matter from a community standpoint.

of only twenty cents of it. If spending becomes insufficient, it will mean that there is income that has been saved and would otherwise lie idle. Then if government borrows it and spends it, the immediate effect is clearly to restore the balance whereby a community renews its income by spending it, instead of failing to spend it all, and therefore failing to renew its income.

It is the aftermath that one has to think about, in the shape of debt and debt charges that have to be met. One answer is that the debt is no burden, so long as the government owes it to its own citizens—we owe it to ourselves. Suppose we borrow one hundred dollars a year to spend on public works, and pay the interest in the approved way, out of added taxes. Then the interest, at three per cent, would mount up in thirty-three and one-third years to one hundred dollars per year, so that our taxes would be as heavy as if we had paid the full one hundred dollars out of taxes from the start, and from then on they would be heavier. We should have deferred the burden on an average less than seventeen years. And we should have piled up a debt of three thousand three hundred thirty-three and one-third dollars to finance an annual outlay of one hundred dollars.

To some of the more advanced thinkers, the convention of laying taxes to pay the interest is a financial superstition, and all we really need is to get rid of it, and be just as ready to borrow to pay the interest as to pay for anything else. If we follow that principle, it will take us less than twenty-four years to reach the point at which the debt has grown to three thousand three hundred thirty-three and one-third dollars, and we are borrowing two hundred dollars a year to keep a public works outlay of one hundred dollars a year going. From then on, we should be disbursing more for interest than for public works, and the disparity would go on increasing as long as we followed that policy. The ultimate goal of endless borrowing, with either method of financing interest, if it went on long enough, would be an economy with a core of real income based on real production, surrounded by a growing volume of fiscal transfer-payments, going to the holders of the public debt. If this were raised by taxes, it could interfere with the willingness to take business risks to expand production; and if it were raised by borrowing, it could create inflationary pressures, while the economy is still short of a satisfactorily high level of employment.

There is one important mitigating factor, namely, the long term growth of the national income. Real income may grow between two per cent and three per cent a year, at the rate we have learned to expect; and if there is also a slow long-term uptrend in prices, moderate enough to be harmless, the total national income, in dollars, might approximately double every twenty years. Then the public debt, and the debt charges, could increase nearly four per cent a year and still maintain an unchanged relation to our national income. This would allow us an annual average deficit of nearly five per cent of a high level national income. Or if there were no increase in prices, the allowable deficit, on this basis, would be about half this size. This would leave considerable elbow room for the kind of policy we have been speaking of, in support of total spending.

One trouble with all this is that we have other uses for this elbow room. Our national debt is already embarrassingly large, and creates difficulties, as we have seen, when conditions call for increases in interest rates. If we do not want to reduce it by way of large surplus revenues, at least it will shrink in relation to the national income if it remains unchanged while the income grows. This is probably the chief way in which the burdens of war debts have been reduced in the past. But if the debt goes on increasing, this method of relative reduction is debarred. The upshot is that there really are difficulties about a mounting public debt, and uneasiness about it is more than an empty superstition; even though it is true that "we owe it to each other," and the interest payments circulate inside our own economy.

If budgets do not have to be balanced, government can save itself the trouble of finding things to spend more money on; it can simply reduce taxes without altering its spending, and leave the taxpayers with more money, most of which they would naturally spend. We have already considered the proposal of a sliding scale of income tax rates, lower in depression and higher in prosperity. If a tendency to depression becomes chronic, and low taxes are continuously used to combat it, this has the same effect on the public debt as the spend-and-borrow policy, and would be open to most of the same objections. Business would become uneasy, and private capital outlays would probably suffer.

From a typical business standpoint, the most desirable method is to reduce both public spending and taxation, in the hope of increasing private spending, both for consumption and capital outlays. This would increase private spending for consumption, but by less than the decrease in public spending. The net effect would depend on whether it increased private capital outlays by more than enough to make up the difference. And of that there could seldom be any assurance.

This does not exhaust the possibilities. There are further questions of the distribution of the spending and of the tax burdens, and there are subsidies and penalties that might be applied as incentives to induce people to do the kind of spending the government wants to bring about. If investment spending by private business were the paramount thing to stimulate, we should naturally make taxes less progressive as well as reduce them. If spending for private consumption is the one decisive thing to be stimulated, we should lighten indirect taxes and make the personal income tax more progressive; in effect shifting disposable income from the high brackets, where a reduction of a dollar might reduce spending by about sixty-two cents, and adding it to the lower brackets, where it might increase spending in the neighborhood of eighty-five to ninety cents. In intermediate brackets, the gain would be smaller, and the average gain in consumer spending, for every dollar shifted, may be roughly and tentatively estimated at twenty cents or a trifle more. Obviously, there is a limit on the amount of income that can be so shifted without seriously interfering with the incentives to private investment spending.[1] Finally, if the kind of spending that seems most in need of support is in the construction industries, and if private construction spending fails to respond, the emphasis will shift to public spending.

Another way in which long-run spending habits may be altered is by changes in the ways in which the future security of individuals is provided for. The individual does it by saving, using two main methods. One is to spend the income from his savings and keep the principal for his heirs—if he can. The other consists of various forms of the annuity method, whereby the principal is consumed, and the saver gets a given amount of personal protection with a smaller long-run increase in the total of saved capital in the society. The annuity principle is making heavy inroads on the other method. Social security is, in principle, a system of annuities, but its financing can be manipulated in the direction of larger or smaller savings by altering the policy of accumulation of reserves. While reserves are being accumulated, the effect is to pull more funds out of circulation than are turned back into it by the payment of benefits, so total spending is decreased, unless this effect is offset, as it has been so far, for the most part, in this country, by public deficits on other accounts. But such a publicly-administered system could be soundly enough conducted without accumulating reserves computed on orthodox actuarial principles. If there were need of increasing consumer spending, the reserves could be reduced; and this might go a long way toward a pay-as-you-go basis, without real danger.

From the standpoint of stimulating private capital outlays, probably the greatest single factor would be an overhauling of the

[1] See Harold Lubell, Effects of Income Redistribution on Consumer's Expenditures, Amer. Econ. Rev., March, 1947, pp. 157–170, and correction, Dec., 1947, p. 930, and J. M. Clark, ibid., p. 931. Strictly speaking, the percentage of their incomes which different income groups spend is not conclusive evidence as to the effect of a change of the sort suggested, but it is the only evidence that seems to be available at present, and probably gives a fair approximation.

tax system, to eliminate features that load the dice against venture-some investment. This would include averaging incomes of good and bad years, carrying losses backward and forward, and some mitigation of the double taxation of corporate income, to the corporation and again to the stockholder. Top-bracket income tax rates might, when practicable, be reduced to, let us say, not more than sixty-five per cent, or less, if genuine peace arrives and fiscal requirements shrink correspondingly. This would, incidentally, set a limit on the effort to increase consumer spending by reducing the inequality of incomes-after-taxes, insofar as this might contemplate making the income tax more steeply progressive at the upper end. But it is still possible, when income taxes can be reduced, to give the greatest relative relief to the low income brackets.

Next to tax reform, many business men would specify a "favorable climate" of government attitude and public opinion, affording business a feeling of the kind of security in which expansion may proceed, subject only to normal business risks. This undoubtedly expresses an important truth; but it is one that, like the "general welfare" or the "forgotten man," means a wide variety of different things to different people. To some, it would call for "sound finance," meaning conventional finance that would veto all or most of the fiscally unconventional devices we have been discussing. To others, ample consumer spending is a major part of a "favorable climate" for business, including a readiness to use well-chosen stimuli when called for, at the expense of traditional fiscal orthodoxy. To some, it might imply relaxation of the antitrust laws; to others, stricter enforcement in the interest of fuller opportunity for small and medium sized independent enterprise. No matter what happens, some of these ideas are due for substantial readjustments.

Back of specific policies, "climate" suggests an underlying attitude which may be fair or prejudiced, favorable or predisposed to hostility. This matter of temper and mood is important in influencing the way in which the economy will respond to policies. Finally, and most important, "climate" is two-sided. Government and business each have a part to play in what needs to be a joint undertaking, and each needs a fair and understanding attitude on the part of the other, if it is to perform its part successfully.

Many business men believe that, given a "favorable climate," voluntary private capital outlays will keep production moving at high speed, without any need for governmental meddling in the attempt to furnish deliberate stimuli or supports. Such a "hands off" policy might bring better results than inept intervention, toward which business adopts a jaundiced attitude—better results meaning prompter recovery when things go wrong. And then again it might not. But to count on it for depression-proof prosperity— that is an act of faith, not warranted by the available evidence. Left to itself, private economic activity will fluctuate; and when it contracts, intervention of some sort has now become inevitable.

For one thing, it is no longer a question of government *versus* no government; if official government kept its hands off, there would still be the unofficial varieties of *de facto* government that have developed within the "private" economic structure, in the councils of big business and trade unions. And they can make mistakes, no less than the Washington brand of politicians. In the next two lectures, some attention will be paid to these possibilities, when we look at price policies and wage policies. There are, perhaps, three main grounds for reasonable hope that future interventions may be helpful, rather than the opposite. First, the next depression is unlikely to be as catastrophic as that of the thirties. Second, statesmen and their advisers have learned something since 1929, and government now includes a body of competent specialists, charged with a continuing task of study and recommendation. Third, business also has learned something, and may respond somewhat more constructively than in the past, to prudently chosen public policies.

12. CONCLUSION

I have made no attempt to deal with all the policies that have been suggested for sustaining the volume of spending. There are others, including proposals to tax idle savings and so push hoarded funds into circulation, and proposals to guarantee demand for particular products. These devices involve serious difficulties, and seem to need a good deal more study before it would be appropriate to push them into the front line of projects contending for early adoption. But the mere fact that they are unorthodox is not in itself a sufficient reason for ruling them out, but merely for treating them with prudent circumspection. Other methods seem at present to be more promising.

On the whole, the prospect we have been surveying is encouraging. As long as we have a system of private enterprise, there will be fluctuations; but we ought to be able to limit them to an endurable magnitude, if we care enough about it to take a good deal of trouble. This may be all we should have to do; the system may not develop any chronic deficiency. But there is a strong chance that it may, and this is one of the possibilities we need to be prepared to deal with. Here there is greater uncertainty as to the effects of particular measures, and more need to feel our way cautiously; but there are promising things we can try, if preconceptions and vested interests do not stand too stiffly in the way of unconventional experimenting.

The job will test all our qualities of social invention and progressive and adaptable citizenship. The outcome cannot be guaranteed. And we certainly are not going to attain perfection in the next ten or twenty years. But we seem to have a fair fighting chance—which is all we deserve or should ask—to maintain a sufficiently high and stable level of demand to give our productive powers the opportunity they need, and to afford Americans the opportunity to earn a bountiful living at productive work, under conditions of justice and freedom that we need not fear to compare with those of any other country. There is no need to remind ourselves that much depends on the outcome.

SOUND STRUCTURE AND BEHAVIOR OF PRICES AND COSTS

1. THE PROBLEM

There are immediate problems of prices, wages and profits which are urgent, but I shall not stress them here, if only for the reason that anything that might be said about them is likely to be "dated" by the time these lectures appear in print. The peculiar force of current inflationary pressures is compounded of temporary postwar readjustments, and of the responses of a system in which both industry and organized labor have large amounts of discretionary power to fix what they will charge for what they have to sell. The more enduring question is: given this kind of industry, and organized labor with this kind of power, what will they make of our price structure over the longer future? More particularly, what will they make of it when the first postwar wave of more-than-ample demand has passed; when we no longer have a market so strong that it can stand almost any kind of pricing, and still call for all the country can produce?

We have already touched on this question, and forecast the conclusion that the best system of prices cannot, of itself, insure stable full employment. On the other hand, there is a strong *prima facie* probability that a bad system can make the task immeasurably more difficult. But what is a "good system" or a "bad system," from this standpoint, and how much difference does it make which we have? By this criterion, is our actual system good, bad or mixed; and if it is imperfect, what can be done to make it less so? If the price system alone cannot carry the whole load, how can it best cooperate with the other measures that are needed? These are some of the questions with which the present lecture will come to grips. We shall not resolve all uncertainties, but we may point the way toward some probable and useful answers.

How far is our actual system competitive, and how far monopolistic? If a competitive system is helpful, and a monopolistic system hurtful, how far do these helpful or hurtful effects go? If a mixed system is inevitable, what are its merits and defects, and how may the defects be minimized? In advance of the argument, it may be suggested that one of the troubles with the attitudes of economic theorists toward competition is to ask too much of it, thereby confusing the effort to make it render the kind of useful service of which it is capable. Another is to judge the defects of the actual working institution by comparison with an unmitigated form which theorists attempt, dimly and partially, to visualize; and to ignore the defects that would appear in unmitigated competition, if it could be actually established.

Are high or low prices better? The question is more misleading than helpful. If either is enduringly established, the system can adjust itself in time, and trade will go on. Or if prices are high in one country, the international exchanges can adjust themselves to this (if they are permitted to do so). What people generally mean when they think of high or low prices is prices higher or lower than the system is adjusted to: in short, the kind of situation that results from change. Changes in international price relations—or perhaps obstructions to needed changes—can disrupt international trade, and the production and employment which depends on it. Or changes in prices without corresponding adjustments in money costs can create unsound conditions within the price structure, which in turn can obstruct production and employment.

So the important thing to look at is movements, and obstructions to movement. But there are many different kinds of movement, short-term and long-term movements in response to changes in costs and in response to changes in demand, movements arising from the relation of particular prices to one another and general movements, which create their own characteristic changes in the relations between different groups or classes of prices. One of the crucial questions is whether, if prices are flexible in response to changes in demand, they can keep production stable when demand fluctuates. If so, they can perhaps do a great deal to forestall the secondary and cumulative fluctuations in demand which, as we saw in the last lecture, are responsible for the most serious extremes of instability. These distinct questions call for individual study; the answer that fits one is inherently unlikely to fit the others.

Moreover, since "costs" are the rewards paid to those who make contributions to production, and since these rewards constitute the incomes of the persons who furnish these contributions, the relative structure of these rewards is important in its own right. This question is not disposed of by the proposition that prices should maintain a proper relation to money costs, because it is not safe to assume that the money costs are properly adjusted. A bad adjustment of wages may force, or be forced by, an undesirable adjustment of prices; and if prices are too ready to adjust themselves to costs, whatever the costs may be, they may permit or facilitate unhealthy wage differentials.

This is a formidable array of questions, and we shall not be able to cover them all. But we may discuss some critical and outstanding threads in this network, and some of their connections with one another.

2. SOME CHARACTERISTICS OF THE PRICE STRUCTURE

There are many kinds of prices. Some are local, some are nation-wide or responsive to conditions in a nation-wide area, and some are international—prices of imported and exported goods, strongly affected by conditions in other countries. Some are made on organized exchanges, some quoted or administered by private producers, some publicly controlled. Prices of perishables and durables respond to different forces and behave in different ways. Some prices are virtually monopolistic and some are exposed to various kinds and degrees of competition, all of which are necessarily "imperfect," in the sense of falling short of the impossible standards that theoretical "perfect competition" has set up. But they are not therefore necessarily useless or seriously unsound.

There are products whose cost of production consists mainly of materials and hired labor, and others in which the work of the producer and his family account for most of the "value added to materials." Farm prices behave differently from those of manufactured products, one of the basic differences being rooted in the fact that the farmer commits himself to a production schedule for a season in advance, without knowing what either the crop yield or the price will be, while the manufacturer is in a position to control his output more or less currently, and to adjust it to the volume of sales he is able to make at the prices he is quoting. The relation of demand and supply may fluctuate because of these seasonal contingencies of supply, which may affect one crop, or farm output in general, over a wide area. Or it may fluctuate because demand has risen or fallen, with fluctuations of income from prosperity to depression, or because a particular industry is growing or permanently declining.

Bound up and interwoven with all these characteristics, there are prices that move sensitively in response to changes in the relation of supply to demand, and prices that are relatively insensitive to such changes, letting them take effect mainly on volume rather than on price. There are technical difficulties of measuring these differences in responsiveness, but the main fact is so clear that not even statistics can cast doubt on it. For some purposes, the important thing is not the movement of a price, but the movement in the producers' margins above costs. Especially crucial are the costs he does not control, and so cannot escape, and the costs he can escape by reducing output and employment. And it is not easy to get a meaningful measure of these various kinds of producers' margins. At the depth of the depression of the thirties, American manufacture was failing to cover operating expenses, though the margin above "direct cost," per dollar of sales, had apparently changed very little. From this general state of facts, different observers draw widely different conclusions, according to interest or temperament.

One of the interesting questions for the future is whether the radical changes in bargaining position which have taken place in the past fifteen years are enough to make the future patterns of behavior different from the past. Fluctuations of agricultural prices have been restricted by governmental price supports, though not enough to wipe out the pattern of sensitiveness to changes of demand or supply. But forces are playing on industrial prices that might end by giving them one-way flexibility, upward only; chiefly because wages have this quality. Organized labor has enough bargaining power to offer very effective resistance to reduction of wage rates when demand falls off, and to raise them when demand revives, by more than the increase in productivity. This means raising unit costs of production at a time when the market is strong enough to enable the producer to recover his increased costs by an increase in price. People are significantly neglecting their opportunities to speak of a "new era" in the postwar period, whether because the term was overworked in the buoyant twenties and discredited by the great depression, or because we do not feel that our succession of crises has emerged into anything as stable or consistent as the word "era" suggests. But if there is a postwar "new era" in prices, this shift toward one-way flexibility may turn out to be one of its distinguishing features.

3. WHAT THE PRICE-COST STRUCTURE DOES

One idea of the functions of the price-cost structure which will stand deflating is the very common conception that it "allocates the country's resources between different uses." This has a basis of truth; but is often wrongly used to support the idea that it takes a change in prices to change the allocation of resources; or the idea that when something is scarce, production will not be stimulated to make good the scarcity unless the price is allowed to go to the full height that supply and demand would dictate. Those in control of large industries do not believe this, and do not practice it, though it has been used as a club to belabor wartime price controls. A moderate shift in resources, increasing the production of this and reducing the production of that, can commonly be brought about simply by changes in the volume of sales, without any change in price. Ultimately, if one of the products is a large factor in the demand for some raw material, the price of this material may change. But, to stimulate an increase in the output of a particular product, a moderate premium above cost is generally sufficient to do all that can usefully be done, and a decrease in output requires no reduction in price.

The principal thing price does, in case of scarcity, is to ration the shortage among different buyers. If the shortage is moderate, and especially if the product is not a necessity, this kind of rationing works well enough and without undue hardship. Often, however, without public intervention, the sellers will practice informal rationing without raising the price to the level that would reduce the demand to match the short supply. And in extreme shortages of necessities, rationing by high prices would concentrate the privation on the low income groups, and give the sellers more gain than would serve any constructive purpose in stimulating production to relieve the shortage. So there comes a point at which we decide to endure the crudities and inconveniences of price control and public rationing, attempting to fix prices consistent with increased production of the scarce necessities, but lower than scarcity would permit producers to fix them.

One further point. Insofar as demand—at a price—allocates resources, it breaks the process up into uncorrelated parts. It does not decide that so many workers shall be shifted out of producing one thing and into producing something else. It decides that so many workers shall cease to produce one thing, and leaves them to decide what to do instead; or it decides that so many more workers shall be sought to increase the output of something else, and leaves open the question where they shall come from. If the pluses and the minuses happen to balance, and if the labor market is efficient and the labor supply mobile, an appropriate movement may result, otherwise it may not. If the pluses and minuses do not balance, then the mechanism we use for allocation will do something more, or something different; it will alter the total amount of utilization of resources, perhaps in a useful direction and perhaps the opposite.

This effect on total production and employment seems to be real and important. But just what it is, and how it works, constitutes one of the difficult frontier problems of economics. Until recently, little or no sound and useful work has been done that was really applicable to it; and most of the recent serious work has been mathematical. It is on this problem that we shall here concentrate, trying to do it in ways that will not be dependent on higher mathematical tools.

4. FLEXIBLE PRICES: DIFFERENT KINDS

Price flexibility is of several kinds which need to be separately considered. There is the adjustment of relative prices, singly, to relative costs; the adjustment of relative prices, singly, to fluctuations in demand and supply; there are fluctuations of a widespread or general character; and there are long-term trends, in which fluctuations in one direction predominate over those in the other direction. Finally, the mere difference between upward and downward movements probably deserves some consideration, for they may be more than simple opposites of one another. Certainly people's attitudes toward them are different, with or without sufficient reason.

5. GENERAL UPWARD FLEXIBILITY: OR "INFLATION"

When upward movements of prices are sufficiently marked and widespread, and especially when they include the prices that do not normally fluctuate much, along with those that habitually move up and down in sensitive fashion, people speak of "price inflation." This is our present problem. The term itself is abused, and means so many different things that it is of doubtful value for precise study. It generally implies a movement that goes beyond the normal cyclical ups and downs, and it is loaded with implications of something bad. And for precise study, the bad effects need to be specified. Where a general price rise does not carry with it any increase in physical production or employment, it is usually taken as a clear case of inflation, though wartime inflation began long before production reached its peak. A general increase may begin at a level generally recognized as too low; and in that case the earlier and more welcome stages may be called "reflation"— which of course does not tell us where reflation ends and (harmful) inflation begins, or how to tell when prices are too low. Presumably it is partly a matter of the relation of prices to costs and partly of the relation of the more sensitive prices to the insensitive ones.

What, then, are the evils of inflation? We may leave on one side inflation of the galloping, astronomical variety, such as afflicts China today, or such as wiped out Germany's currency after the first World War. It would be a catastrophe, and the prospect of its happening to this country is remote at present. At the other extreme, there is no harm in a moderate upward swing of the more sensitive wing of prices, of a sort that can easily be reversed if conditions of demand change. And there is probably no harm in a slow long-term upward drift averaging, let us say, not more than one and one-half per cent or perhaps two per cent per year, combined with shorter fluctuations in such a way that it would not be easily identified as an established long-term trend. It would reduce the value of savings, but not drastically, and would benefit the holders of equity claims to income. It would make venture capital a little more profitable, on the average of good and less good times. If it were identifiable as a steady upward trend, the rate of interest on loans might rise in such a way as to offset the annual reduction in the buying power of the principal, and cancel the advantage accruing to the borrower and equity investor; but when the long-term rise is compounded with shorter ups and downs, this is not likely to happen. Such a slow, irregular upward movement of prices has apparently been the prevailing historical trend for many centuries, though perhaps it has been too irregular for the best results; periods of no uptrend alternating with periods when fairly rapid inflation benefited trading interests and the manufacturing entrepreneurs of the period, but laid a heavy burden on wage earners, whose wages fell far behind the rise of prices, in the days before organized labor was an established factor to be reckoned with.

It is in these shorter and sharper movements that the evils of inflation are to be sought. It is often said that inflation is bad because it leads to a subsequent slump. The difficulty here is to distinguish the effects of the movement of prices from the movement of demand, production and employment with which it is associated. A general boom may lead to a slump in activity, but will it, under the kind of conditions we may expect in the future, lead to a slump in prices? And how much worse is the general fluctuation made by the movement of prices that accompanies it? The movements of prices do undoubtedly contribute some speculative elements, plus and minus, leading to accentuation of the physical ups and downs, but these are probably of secondary importance, compared to the main causes of the movements. And the price movements create injustices, falling unevenly on different groups. But under present conditions, the danger may be not so much that a wave of inflation will lead to a subsequent slump in prices as that this feature of the slump will be effectively resisted.

And as a result, the long-term upward drift will be speeded up to a rate that might be seriously disturbing.

Inflation reduces the burden of the public debt, but it does so at the expense of the bondholder. If the reduction in the value of his principal is less than the interest he receives, he still gets some return, though less than he contracted for; if it is greater, his return is turned into an absolute loss. This has happened, for example, to the present Series E bonds—the four dollars which the bondholder is to receive at maturity is already, in most cases, worth less than the three dollars he paid for his bond was worth at the time he subscribed. The same shrinkage has occurred in the values of insurance policies, annuities and retirement pensions. From this standpoint, an annual inflation of two per cent might be tolerable, but four per cent robs the saver. This defines one of the critical points at which inflation begins to be a serious evil.

If we go far beyond this, a further point is reached at which people begin to distrust the value of money, even for a short time, and try to get rid of it, converting it into goods or equities. This "flight from money" ushers in rapid and unlimited inflation. It is usually associated with a government that is unable to come near balancing its budget. We seem to be in no danger of reaching this point, but it is worth keeping in mind. When there is an excess of buying power active in the markets, price inflation does not "absorb" it, as is frequently said, it merely pushes it around from hand to hand at a speedier rate.

The causes of inflation may be roughly divided into two, the pull of excess spending and the push of rising money costs, with the familiar "spiral" that results when they combine, with money costs—chiefly wages—chasing prices and forcing prices up, so that the pursuit has no easily definable end. First, as to the "pull." When people spend beyond the income of the immediate past, this generates an increase in present dollar income. If it also generates an equal increase in physical output of goods, there need be no inflation, though there may be an unhealthy expansion, of a sort that cannot be sustained, for reasons already touched on. Even if there is more money looking for goods than goods looking for buyers, that does not automatically raise prices, except those that are made on organized exchanges; it merely makes it possible for them to be raised. Producers are likely to take advantage of this possibility, though not generally to the full extent that demand permits. They may bid up the prices of materials, and raise the prices of finished products enough to increase their profit margins.

The next move is likely to be an increase in wages. In the long run, if wages increase no more than productivity, the labor cost of production per unit of output is not increased, and prices are not forced up, except to the extent that prices of materials may have risen. From the side of wages, the inflationary pushing up of prices comes when hourly money wages rise more than output per man-hour. In the long run, increased productivity makes possible continuous increase in the real buying power of wages, and it is the only major source from which such an increase can come. Wages may expand at the expense of profits by absorbing a larger percentage share of the total product of industry, or they may expand at the farmer's expense if they rise faster than his share does—as they did in the period between the first and second World Wars. At a time when profits are high and when agriculture is booming, there may be some room for labor to pull up its share by sheer bargaining power, and there is always a chance for a particular group of workers to score individual gains. But for labor as a whole, in ordinary times, these sources are not to be counted on. The farmer cannot be squeezed further without serious consequences, and if normal profits are encroached on, they will tend to reestablish themselves by way of increased prices, thus neutralizing any wage increases gained by such encroachment. Under such conditions, wage increases in excess of productivity become an active inflationary force, pushing prices up in a spiral that could be endless.

Ordinarily, with increasing productivity, weekly earnings can more than keep pace with the cost of living; but special conditions can arise in which this is temporarily impossible, and then wage increases will be self defeating, and will serve to push the cost of living up. The cost of living may rise because booming demand has raised the prices of raw produce, or weekly earnings may shrink because of a reduction in hours worked without offsetting increase in productivity per hour. Both these things happened at the end of the war, resulting in a condition which could not be overcome merely by raising money rates of wages. In such a case, the "vicious inflationary spiral" becomes an active force, until the shortage is absorbed by increased productivity, or by some of the participating groups acquiescing in a shrinkage of real income. Only then can the spiral be expected to come to an end, possibly at a permanently increased level of prices.

As to remedies, they need to be adapted to the character and causes of the particular inflationary situation, and to be used with discrimination. They fall under four general heads, according to whether they operate through the total level of spending relative to production, through the pressures that act on the profit margins of business, through the pressures that act on the wage bargain, or through direct control of prices and wages, with allocation and rationing of scarce and critical items. Direct controls are a story by themselves. They have so far been reserved for temporary use in extreme emergencies; and they will presumably not come into more general use unless other methods fail dismally.

As to control through the volume of spending, we have been discussing ways of stabilizing spending, or of sustaining it if it becomes insufficient. To deal with inflation, the sustaining policy would need to be thrown into reverse gear, but not indiscriminately. Taxation might be increased, but not the kind that can be shifted by raising prices. Credit would need to be restricted; but with care not to restrict the kind of credit that is used to increase the supply of goods, especially at "bottleneck" points, where the supply can be increased and the bottlenecks eased. The kind of credit that needs restricting is the kind that increases demand without increasing supply, including consumer credit and business credit that would merely increase demand for unavoidably scarce materials. Control of credit needs to be wisely selective. Or government can undertake to borrow to mop up excessive buying power, as it is attempting to do at present; but it is hard to make a low-interest bond attractive as an investment, when the principal is so likely to lose buying power faster than the interest can make it up.

When political or military necessity, or both, call for extraordinary expenditures, it may be impracticable, economically as well as politically, to levy the drastic taxes and carry out the other measures that are necessary to prevent an inflationary excess of purchasing power from arising. Then, if the country is not ready to turn to strong direct controls, it must rely for avoidance of serious inflation on the complex of intangible forces that go to determine profit margins and wage rates. Short of direct controls, we seem to depend mainly on competition to keep down profit margins, and on employers' resistance to keep wage increases within moderate bounds. But in both cases, we seem to be entering a phase in which informal pressures of public policy are playing an increasing role. We shall presently be paying some attention to these matters, but first we have a further major question to examine as to what kind of price behavior is desirable, and how effective it can be.

6. DOWNWARD FLEXIBILITY OF PRICES AS A RESTORATIVE FOR WEAKENED DEMAND—HOW EFFECTIVE CAN IT BE?

There is no question that prices should be flexible enough to maintain a suitable relation to costs, on the average of good and bad times, either for single industries or for industry as a whole. Postponing the question of just what a "suitable relation" is; if it has once been established, major changes in costs should lead to adjustments that would restore normal margins; and changes in the costs of particular commodities should be reflected in their prices, relative to others. And there is no question that a single industry can, in general, sell more of its product at a lower price than at a higher one, though there may be doubt whether the increase is enough to outweigh the reduction of price and to increase the dollar volume of sales. But when we come to the effect of a reduction of price on the total demand for things in the economy, we face a more stubborn and difficult question, and the analogy of single prices is an undependable guide.

When a single price is reduced, one product has been made cheaper, and the amount of income available to buy it (and to buy other things) has not been much affected. Whatever effect there may be on the general state of demand for other things is slight and diffused, and can properly be disregarded. But a general reduction of prices, or of prices and wages, is a different matter, and the effect on incomes becomes as important as the effect on the cost of acquiring goods. Every change in price affects someone's income from the sale of a unit of the commodity by precisely as much as it affects the outlay necessary to buy it; and the two effects could easily cancel out. Or if they do not precisely cancel, it is on account of things like leads, lags, shifts in the distribution of income and of demand between persons and groups, or effects on expectations; and the net balance of effect is far from clear and obvious. So there are theories that if prices were only flexible enough, this would maintain demand at a full employment level; and theories that it would be useless for this purpose or even harmful.

In the case of wages, the conflict is even more absolute. The next time unemployment becomes a conscious problem, we may be sure that some will propose wage increases as a remedy, to sustain demand for labor by sustaining buying power; and others will argue that wages (as costs of employing labor) are too high to permit full employment, and that some of them at least should come down. This contradiction exhibits in practical form the fallacy of reasoning from the particular to the general, and forces us to face the more difficult problem of over-all effects. Systematic study of this problem is still in its infancy.

One theory concentrates on the conception that a general reduction of prices means that people's cash balances will have more power to buy goods. In real terms, they will increase, and these increases will have some tendency to push themselves into circulation by buying an increased physical volume of goods.[1] The theory presupposes that the actual volume of cash balances does not decline as fast as prices do, and that the volume people are willing to hold tends, among other things, to hold some normal relation to the dollar volume of transactions which these balances have to finance.

Any realistic solution of this theory must go beyond the old classroom fantasy which described everyone waking up some morning to find every coin in his pocket doubled—presumably in a system with no banks and no Fort Knox. We must reckon with the realities and mysteries of a modern banking system. And one of these realities is the fact that, when the dollar volume of transactions shrinks, the volume of bank balances shrinks with it, though not instantly and not in exact proportion. And we must reckon with the further question whether, if ample real cash balances have some effect in sustaining the volume of buying, this effect can be brought about in other and less disturbing ways than by a general fall in prices.

If bank deposits do shrink, this means that banks have excess reserves, and this makes for easy credit and low interest rates. This would have a tendency to stimulate borrowing for capital outlays, and possibly also toward fuller use of consumer credit, if it went far enough to affect the terms granted on installment loans. But the evidence points to the conclusion that this is not a powerful enough incentive to offset the forces of an economic

[1] Mr. Gardiner C. Means has developed this theory in a book which is now in preparation. Mr. Means should not be held responsible for any interpretation I may give of this theory.

recession, and to drive idle banking resources into full use. More-over, as we have seen, under present conditions there is little room for interest rates to decline farther than they already have. This remedy has some force, but must be judged partial and inadequate.

Banking policy has another weapon, in the shape of buying securities in the open market, and so increasing the available cash resources, either in the hands of banks or in those of individuals. If people want to take funds and use them, and are prevented by the limits of their existing bank balances, this method may loosen the restriction and permit a larger volume of spending. But there is doubt whether it has much power to force funds into use if people do not already want to use them. In such a case, those who have sold securities to the government will be more likely to want to reinvest the funds than to spend them directly, and the immediate effect may be mainly to sustain the prices of stocks, rather than to increase demand for goods. This remedy also appears to be partial and inadequate, where the disease consists of an insufficient willingness to take funds and put them into active use.

To return to the effect of price reductions, granting that check-ing accounts shrink, largely through the repayment of loans which are not required for the shrunken volume of business, they still do not generally shrink as much as the volume of business does, with the result that they remain large, relative to current require-ments, as shown in a reduction in their "velocity of circulation." It is fair to assume that people have some tendency to put these unnecessary balances to some use—not everyone is likely to be content to leave them virtually idle. But what use? Will they spend more for consumption—more, that is, than their current incomes would dictate? Probably not to any great extent. Some will be forced into that course by necessity; but their balances are small and will soon be exhausted. Others will be mainly governed by their shrunken current incomes. They are more likely to hunt some kind of investment, in an economy in which capital outlays by business have ceased to seem inviting, and the climate is unfavorable to a stockmarket boom. The indicated conclusion is that this kind of induced spending is not likely to get very far, If, as seems likely, only a minor fraction of the idle real buying power is automatically pushed into active use, then it follows that, to neutralize a shrinkage of, let us say, five to ten per cent in total buying, by reduction of prices, prices would have to fall, at best, by several times this percentage. And such a violent fall in prices has its own discouraging effects on business buying. On the whole, then, there are strong reasons for skepticism as to the power of a general price reduction to counteract a business recession.

There remain the questions of the relations of prices to one another and to costs. Prices of raw materials are more flexible than those of finished products, and a reduction in these prices reduces the direct cost of production of the finished products. This may make possible a large or small reduction in the final price, depending on whether materials are the principal element, or a minor one, in total cost (including cost of distribution); and in any case it is subject to the counteracting effect of increased unit costs due to reduced output. Perhaps this last ought not to influence price policy, since it is mainly due to spreading the overhead over smaller volume, and does not greatly affect the added cost of added output; but as prices are actually made, business men do take total cost per unit into account, and this further limits the reduction of prices to the final purchaser. The general result is that the reduction of prices, considered by itself, reduces the real buying power of producers of raw materials, and slightly mitigates the shrinkage elsewhere in the economy, with business likely to absorb much of the benefit. So far, the over-all effect is still not clear.

If wages also are reduced, and if this reduction is passed on to the purchaser, some of the benefit would presumably reach the producers of raw materials, and mitigate their disadvantage. But the immediate over-all effect is still a doubtful balance between a reduction of cost to the purchaser and reduction of his income, per unit of product. We will consider this question further in the next lecture; for the time being, we may simply assume that wages are strongly resistant to such deflation.

There is also the question of our exports. At lower prices, the foreign buyer can buy more of our products than at higher ones; and this may bring an increase in the total amount of goods purchased. For some small countries, heavily dependent on foreign trade, this is an important factor; but for us it represents a comparatively small mitigation of the impact of a general recession.

Finally, there are producers' margins. If they are reduced, and the benefit passed on in lower prices, the immediate effect is likely to include a net balance of increase in consumer buying. The effect on capital outlays is more doubtful. There will be more need to replenish inventories, but there may be little incentive to do more. A net increase in capital outlays depends on a multitude of considerations, which may be summed up under three heads. Producers must expect that demand will revive and that profitable margins will be restored. They must feel that now is an advantageous time to increase inventories, or to modernize their plants or provide capacity for future expansion. And they must be able to find funds or get them on good terms. An extreme slashing of margins might make financing difficult; short of that, the effect is likely to be favorable. To state the obvious, a good· deal depends on whether the margins were unnecessarily high to start with. Actually, margins above direct costs, per unit of product, seem to be even more strongly resistant than wage rates to reduction in a recession. This high degree of rigidity is presumably unfortunate. But it might be even more unfortunate if margins were squeezed so low that producers are discouraged or prevented from making capital outlays which they would otherwise be willing to make. There is some point beyond which a dollar saved to purchasers by reduction of sellers' margins would reduce real expenditures and not increase them, including its effect in curtailing capital outlays.

This is easy to say, but it remains difficult for anyone to determine where the critical point comes in practice. We have been discussing the sort of difficulty that is often covered by the elusive and magic word "maladjustments." There is naturally no simple formula for determining precisely what division of the proceeds between extractive industry, manufacturing and distribution, or between wages and profits, will lead to the largest possible amount of physical production and employment. Industry is going to need, in its own interest, to pay high real wages and accept moderate profit margins. But it is a commonplace—or should be—that there is some minimum limit below which profit-margins cannot be pinched without defeating the end in view by curtailing the vitally important sector of spending that consists of capital outlays made in view of a prospective return. Somewhere lies a desirable balance.

One of the obstacles to expanding demand by reducing prices consists in what we may call the "curse of the reverse effect," which comes into play when a reduction of price leads potential buyers to think that prices are likely to go still lower, with the result that they hold off for a better bargain, and temporarily buy less instead of more. There are two ways of combating this difficulty which might be effective; one involving regimentation of particular prices, the other, stabilization of the general range within which prices fluctuate. The first we are unlikely to accept, the second is far from easy or certain to succeed.[1]

[1] There is a third suggestion, which is not applicable to the price structure as a whole: namely, that the "curse of the reverse effect" does not apply to the kind of prices that are made on markets of the produce-exchange type, because here the price at any time registers the traders' estimates of all probable future changes. It may be questioned whether this wholly gets rid of the "curse," even for prices that can be made by this kind of trading. Many industrial buyers are still left in a position in which they might construe an initial movement of the market as a premonitory symptom of more to come, or as confirming other symptoms that point in this direction.

To be fully effective, a price reduction should move fairly quickly about as far as it is going to move at all. In addition, it should probably move to a level from which it is depended on to rise again, when demand revives. The first would require controlled fluctuations, not the kind of tentative and uncertain movements characteristic of uncontrolled competition. A strong private monopoly could manipulate prices in this controlled fashion, if it chose to do so; but most industries with some degree of quasi-monopoly power appear on the whole to prefer price stability to this kind of deliberate fluctuation. And the public is not likely to welcome private monopolistic price control, even if wisely exercised. If the public were to undertake to bring about this kind of flexibility by direct price controls, it would be adopting a kind of policy contrary to all our traditions of public price control, which work toward even greater rigidity than prevails in private industry, and which protect industry's "fair return" in a way that would require constitutional changes before effective reductions in a depression could be enforced.

The alternative seems to be to strengthen competition, causing it to act more promptly and drastically, but setting up general conditions that would afford some underlying stability, and perhaps something like a floor below which the general level of prices would not drop. There are various ways of promoting this result. Government might make money easy and plentiful, or it might undertake expanded public works or other kinds of spending; but it is not likely deliberately to delay these measures until prices have scored what is judged to be the correct amount of decline. If this happened, it would probably be by chance, because the policies did not take effect as promptly as desired. One thing that might come close to setting a floor on prices would be successful resistance of unions to any wage reductions, presumably coupled with price floors for agricultural products. This would mean that the impact of price reductions would be concentrated on profit margins. A small price decline, absorbed out of profits, could have some sustaining effect on the level of real buying, especially by consumers; but it could not go very far without threatening the volume of capital outlays seriously enough to cancel its good effects.

Perhaps the underlying dilemma here is that, without manipulation, price flexibility is bound to have the tentative and uncertain character which brings about the "reverse effect"; and with manipulation, confidence in an underlying normal level of prices tends to be undermined, while the uncertainty is likely to be merely shifted to the question when the manipulated price movements are going to be put into effect. For some kinds of prices, particular kinds of bargains may partly resolve this dilemma—for instance, public works contracts might be made contingent on given price reductions, after which the volume of public works demand might be sufficient to stabilize prices in this area against further downward pressure, and the reduction might cause some revival of private construction. Of more general application is the practice of making forward contracts which guarante the buyer that he will be given the benefit of any subsequent price reduction. But if this becomes general in any industry, it greatly reduces the sellers's incentive to make any further reduction, and probably, on the whole, tends more to sustain price stability than to promote flexibility. To sum up, the "reverse effect" can be reduced, but hardly eliminated.

If it is not practicable or useful to make all prices flexible, that suggests the question: with which commodities can flexibility do the most good? One obvious answer is: "those of elastic demand, whose physical volume of sales responds most strongly to price, so that the dollar volume is higher at lower prices." This answer encounters two difficulties. One is that there is no good way of determining with anything like precision which commodities have elastic demands, and most producers seem to think that the demands for their own commodities are inelastic. The other is that we are concerned, not merely with the effect on demand for these particular commodities, but on demand in general, with the result that the analysis needs to go a good deal farther.

Most goods of high elasticity are probably so because a reduction in their prices, other things remaining the same, makes people buy more of them and less of something else which is in a broad sense a substitute. If we made up groups of commodities which have this kind of relation to one another, demand for any single commodity in each group would exhibit high elasticity if its price changed and the others in the group did not. But if the prices of all the commodities in one group changed about equally, this would probably not reveal any specially high elasticity for the group as a whole. It would not make people buy more of this group and less of other groups.

If we could conceive of a general price reduction with dollar incomes unchanged, that would be logically similar to the effect of an increase in dollar incomes, with prices unchanged. And a good deal is known about the response of buying to changes in dollar incomes, for major groups of commodities. Total consumer buying follows dollar incomes very closely, with basic necessities less elastic than the average, and other things more elastic; and there is some reason for thinking that these groups would show the same kind of difference in response to a general price change. But this, after all, is beside the point. If the price of an inelastic commodity is reduced, people buy little more of it, and spend less for it, but have more left to spend on other things. If the price of an elastic commodity is reduced, people buy more of it and spend more on it, so they have less left to spend on other things. Therefore the effect on over-all demand is likely to be about as great in one case as in the other.

Are price reductions likely to be more useful in consumers' goods or in things like steel, machinery and factory construction —things bought by businesses for enlargements of capital? In trying to answer this, one must distinguish different kinds and degrees of price reductions. Consider, first, price reductions absorbed by business out of its profit margins, without reducing wages. Such reductions would necessarily be rather small. The most important question is whether, if they come fairly early in a recession, they can help to stop the decline. The answer seems to be that such reductions on capital goods would have virtually no effect of this preventive sort. It is generally accepted by students of business cycles that when a recession gets under way, the demand for capital goods is inelastic, until the recession has spent itself. When recovery is around the corner, such price reductions might help it to come a little sooner and perhaps with a little more vigor, but they would not prevent the recession from running most of its course.

Small reductions in things consumers buy—shoes and shirts and automobiles—would have some slight effect in sustaining buying, and the benefit would be evenly distributed among consumers. But that very fact would mean that it would not go where it was most needed. In a recession, some people's incomes do not shrink at all, and others shrink one hundred per cent; they lose their jobs. If business is ready to make a contribution to prosperity out of reduced profit margins, the same amount would be more effective if it were added to unemployment benefits.

Larger reductions in prices would require some reductions in wages, and then the question takes a different shape. Here it is the consumer goods in which a price reduction is futile, if it carries with it a corresponding reduction of wages. It reduces buying power as much as it reduces the cost of goods. And it is capital goods in which a really substantial reduction might do something to revive or sustain demand, even if wages have to be reduced, since a reduction in wages in these industries would not do much to impair the demand for their products, which comes mostly from other industries, and would make it possible to offer a real bargain price. Even this might not be enough, in itself, to induce business to make capital expansions in advance of need, for reasons already suggested. But if an integrated program were worked out, aimed at stabilized capital outlays, a bargain price might be an essential and effective part of it.

The most important goods to stimulate, from the standpoint of keeping the economic mechanism running under a good head of steam, are goods that promote a changed way of living, which is fairly sure to carry with it demands for a good many other things. For example, automobiles and good roads promote one another, and both together have relocated population and brought about an enormous amount of new construction of many sorts. Perhaps a nation of philosophers would wish to reduce their material wants rather than increase them; but we are not such philosophers. Even so, a nation that is merely prudent might want to set some competent minds at work appraising the probable secondary consequences of major innovations and preparing to go to meet them, rather than having them arrive unannounced and unexpected. But these are matters of long-run policy, and seem to shed no new light on questions of flexible prices in depressions. As to that, we have looked at most of the arguments, and what we found may help to explain why economists are at present increasingly skeptical as to the effectiveness of price-flexibility as a way of stabilizing employment and physical production.

It is a question on which pure theory can reach few positive conclusions. Perhaps the most useful clue is the effect of timing. If something has both plus and minus effects, but the plus ones —which are also the more direct and obvious ones—come first, they may gain a momentum that neutralizes part of the minus effects, and leaves a positive net balance. This may be one of the principal reasons for retaining some remnants of optimism as to the efficacy of price flexibility of some sorts and under some conditions. But it warrants only a cautious and conditional optimism, contingent on a showing that the conditions are favorable.

7. PRICE FLEXIBILITY AND WHAT ELSE?

What seems needed is a combined program, in which various kinds of private and public arrangements for stabilizing demand are facilitated by price flexibility, and in which these arrangements serve in turn to make price flexibility safer for the economy, by moderating a decline in demand and affording some assurance that a resulting decline in prices will not go to destructive lengths. Perhaps one of the chief reasons for not abandoning the idea of price flexibility is not so much its good effects—we have seen that by itself it is an uncertain and even a risky form of economic medicine —but rather the fact that it is one of the natural accompaniments of strong and active competitive pressure on prices, and that is desirable, for obvious reasons. So what is needed is an economic mechanism in which strong and active competitive pressure will act within reasonably safe limits, and will not be disastrous for business health. There are many difficulties in the way of such an outcome, both practical and legal difficulties, but if its importance is fully recognized by all concerned, in business, labor and government, and if they are all willing to modify their established habits and cooperate in good faith, a good deal might be accomplished.

The simplest arrangement of this sort would be a contract between an industrial enterprise and a concern supplying it with construction work or long-lived capital equipment, in which the buyer gets a special discount in return for regularizing his buying, or doing a minimum amount of it in slack times. But to be effective, such arrangements would need to be extended vertically until substantially all items in the cost of the capital equipment were included in arrangements of the same sort. Otherwise, the supplier would not be able to give a large enough concession in price to outweigh the various disadvantages of stabilized buying, which have already been discussed. And such a network of contracts, besides being hard to bring about, might have the effect of tying each buyer to a single supplier, to an extent which would be a substantial restraint on competition.

An undertaking on the part of one buyer to deliver a steady volume of orders to one supplier would not necessarily do anything to stabilize total volume. The buyer might give the one supplier only as much business as he could maintain as a minimum, and take the fluctuating excess elsewhere. And most industrial concerns are not sure enough of their own future to be able to give anything like an assurance, much less a positive guarantee, of steady capital requirements. Of course, if capital requirements in general were made steadier, that would make consumer demand steadier, and this would mean a further, cumulative steadying of capital requirements. But the fortunes of competition and shifting demand might still plunge any particular producer into difficulties in which any capital outlays would be unwise, even at a reduced price. Some leading producers are sure enough of their position to undertake some degree of this kind of responsibility; but it is hard to imagine it becoming the general rule, unless industry were organized in cartels, and single producers were assured their quotas.[1]

Some of the proposals that have been made for government guarantee of demand for products have a kind of limited price flexibility about them. That is, these plans propose that, if a producer gives an advance undertaking to produce a given amount, the government will undertake to take any unsold surplus off his hands, typically at a price that would save him from loss but afford no profit. This would put a floor under prices, but it seems highly uncertain what effect it would have on their behavior above this floor. Will it tend toward lower prices by increasing the supply of goods? (It would increase demand too, by increasing

[1] The reader will recall the discussion in the previous lecture (p. 101, above) of suggestions that the government, rather than individual suppliers, might be a party to such arrangements, and might offer an incentive to buyers to time their purchases to promote stabilization.

the income disbursed for materials and labor, but seldom by the exact amount of the increase in supply.) Or would it tend to make producers hold their prices more stiffly, because they could always dispose of their surplus? Or would it work in different ways in different industries? The government would surely be unwilling to absorb surpluses brought about by the maintenance of unreasonably high prices; on the other hand, if it made its guarantee conditional on the producer's price falling to the guaranteed level, the guarantee would be worthless. And if it set some intermediate level, then it would be controlling prices, with a possible escape for the producers if they were free to throw up their guarantee at any time.

We cannot follow out all the contingencies of such a proposal. The most obvious difficulties are those the government would face in disposing of the surplus in ways that would not compete in the producers' regular market. But if these are solved or disregarded, clearly there are still troublesome complications as to the behavior of prices under such a plan. It would change the character of the problem of price flexibility, rather than solve it.

In some fields, where government is a large buyer, it is in a position to influence the course of prices; especially in the construction industry if it sustains it with public works when private demand falls off. In a severe depression, it might become the chief buyer, and be in a position to use bargaining leverage for price reductions. But all its established practices drive instead toward the pegging of prices. There are legal provisions which maintain going rates of wages on public works, even when these rates are being unofficially shaded on private work. And the practice of public bidding often defeats its own end, because the bidders will not shade their regularly published prices in such a public way, though they might be ready to do so in private transactions. So the government may pay more than others are paying, not less. It is alleged that, when a low bid is received, the low bidder sometimes finds that others have been given the chance to meet his bid and share the business, thus reducing his incentive to underbid on subsequent transactions. If all bids seem too high, it is possible to reject them and repeat the bidding process; but this is cumbersome, and does not always produce the desired result. There are, of course, reasons for this mechanical procedure; it serves as a safeguard against favoritism or outright corruption on the part of purchasing agents, and there can be no denying that there is need for such safeguards. But there is also need for greater bargaining discretion, despite its dangers.

The question at issue is part of a much larger one. It seems that government cannot escape the necessity of playing an active part in the market, as part of its new responsibility for policies stabilizing economic fluctuations. This inevitably involves an amount of administrative discretion far beyond anything contemplated by the nineteenth-century theory and practice of government. This discretion involves things that affect private business interests on a great scale, and affords numberless openings for undue and improper influence. Unless the government can maintain its integrity reasonably well in the face of these pressures, it simply will not succeed in doing its necessary job in the coming decades.

Perfection is not to be expected, and is not the issue. The issue is one of the relative importance of what the country might gain through freer administrative discretion, as compared to what might be gained by maintaining old-fashioned checks in all their rigor. To make the latter kind of gain paramount, whatever else happens, seems to involve a serious warping of perspective, under the conditions we now face. It could easily prove penny-wise and pound-foolish. We should not abandon all checks, but we need to judge them by a revised standard. Safety in economic policies has acquired new yardsticks.

Price flexibility on public contracts may not be of enormous importance by itself, though it would enable limited appropriations to give more employment. Probably the chief benefit that might come from it would come if it brought corresponding reductions on private contracts; and this in turn would be important only in connection with programs or arrangements for regularized private capital outlays. In short, piecemeal measures seem likely to be relatively ineffective; important results hinge on a rounded and integrated policy, in which price reductions might play a part, but would not be the sole reliance.

8. POLICY TOWARD MONOPOLY AND COMPETITION

In the short time remaining, it will be possible only to touch too briefly on a few outstanding features of this large problem. In the first place the important thing is that business should run on as a low a profit margin as its health will allow, but no lower. Genuine monopolistic profiteering, and the restriction of output that goes with it, can be serious obstacles to high-level employment, as well as to equitable division of the national income. We may take for granted that antitrust policy will be maintained. But that is negative. The positive side of policy must emphasize the conditions necessary to healthy competition, starting with recognition that all practicable forms of competition are "imperfect," and that the "perfect competition" of economic theory is academic. Doctrinaire insistence on perfection, in competition or in antitrust policy, is a mistake.

Antitrust policy is being pushed in the direction of increasing emphasis on the control of trade practices, but in negative fashion, by "cease-and-desist" orders. This raises the question whether positive administrative supervision of trade practices would not be more logical, and carry more responsibility for canvassing the probable results of the actions taken. But the authorities are rightly reluctant to assume these enormous responsibilities, for some obvious reasons. It is easier to tell people to stop what they are doing than to tell them what to do instead. It takes less wisdom, less resourcefulness, less complete knowledge of the industry.

There is an additional consideration, rooted in a characteristic of competition which may not be so obvious: namely, a tendency for trade practices to become stereotyped, and for competitive pressures to weaken and bog down, as each rival learns what to expect of the others. Contrary to the theoretical idea that "perfect competition" requires perfect knowledge, effective competition may in practice require some salutary uncertainty, such as goes with novelty. It is possible that the energy of competition depends on the arrival, now and then, of new kinds and areas of trade contact, new technical methods, new products, new personalities able to try new policies—all acting to jar practices out of the ruts into which they tend to settle. Positive administrative control of trade practices would add to this stereotyping tendency, whereas an occasional "cease-and-desist" order might have an opposite effect, forcing the members of the industry to experiment with new practices. This may in itself be a negative advantage, arising from precisely the feature that makes it a hardship for the concern that has to try to figure out what kind of conduct the order permits. This hardship in some cases reaches the point of injustice. So one would hardly advocate issuing a blanket "cease-and-desist" order every ten years, merely on the ground that things need stirring up. The "stirring-up" principle, like many others, is not one to push to an ultimate logical extreme.

Healthy competition has somehow to reconcile two conditions. First, it must promote a distribution of incomes consistent with the kind of mass demand for goods on which our system is dependent. For this purpose, profit margins must be narrow and total profits moderate. Second, it must allow the most efficient enterprises profits enough to induce them to expand, while the least efficient are being weeded out, but not weeded out so fast as to put a large portion of industry into bankruptcy. Industry can be healthy with ten to fifteen per cent of its output produced at a loss.[1] But if this were doubled or tripled, it would mean crisis: something industry

[1] "Bulk-line cost" studies, first made at the time of the first World War, have indicated this as a normal percentage.

could live through if it did not last more than a few years, but inconsistent with health if maintained as a steady diet. To satisfy both the first and second conditions requires a proper amount of difference in costs of production, not too much and not too little, between the low-cost producers who lead the procession and the high-cost producers who bring up the rear and are in danger of dropping out.

The natural tendency is for differences in cost to be too great, by this standard, especially among small concerns, which show a wider dispersion of costs than do large concerns. Where that is true, it means that, in order to avoid an unduly large percentage of deficits, total profits must be larger than is necessary to induce healthy expansion; and any unnecessarily large total profits involve some risk of making the distribution of incomes top-heavy. Remedies for this dilemma include aids to efficiency for small producers, guidance as to available openings, perhaps aids to obtaining capital, always provided that the other conditions are good enough to make access to capital a real benefit and not a mere trap for the unwary—a way of leading too many people into ventures foredoomed to failure. Possibly ways can be found of affording wider access to the stock of technical knowledge protected by massed patents, without damaging the institution of patents for the purposes it is designed to serve. Ways may be found for reducing various privileges or advantages which large business often has over smaller business, and which are irrelevant to inherent efficiency. It is axiomatic that the health and efficiency of small business is a key to a successful competitive system, and it will not take care of itself automatically.

9. CONCLUSION

In conclusion, we have been exploring into the question of the effects of the price structure and its behavior on the total amount of production and employment. We have found enough to indicate that these effects are important, but that we can learn comparatively little about them by traditional kinds of analysis, based on the law of supply and demand for single products. For that purpose the most important thing seems to be a good balance in the distribution of the national income between wages and profits, between rich and poor, between consumer spending and saving. A bad price-cost structure may mean failure; a good one may not be enough in itself to insure success, it may be necessary but not sufficient. And its chief effectiveness may be as a complementary part of some more comprehensive policy or program. Among such programs, there are no panaceas easily evident; but there are promising lines of work for people who are ready to cooperate, to make concessions and to depart from conventional patterns, wherever sufficient reason appears.

COLLECTIVE BARGAINING AND WAGES

1. DUAL CHARACTER OF COLLECTIVE BARGAINING

Collective bargaining has become, with surprising swiftness, one of the greatest forces in our society. In anything like its present scale and power, it is a new thing. It has its constructive side, and its disruptive side; and a sound American economy hinges, to an extent hardly possible to exaggerate, on how well this great force is assimilated, and whether it develops mainly in constructive or disruptive directions.

We start with two propositions. First, collective bargaining with strong unions is not only inevitable, it is indispensable. As I have said elsewhere, it is the worker's alternative to serfdom.[1] Second, collective bargaining as now practiced introduces monopolistic determination of the terms of employment, the principal element in the cost and the price of most things. And that makes it inconsistent with a competitive economy. Many people can see one or the other of these propositions. It is harder to see both, and hardest of all to see how they can be fitted together. Yet a healthy economy requires some tolerable and workable resolution of this incompatibility. It must obviously be an imperfect adjustment, and almost as obviously a moving and changing one. This difficulty I shall try to look squarely in the face. I shall consider it in an evolving framework that starts with prevailingly private enterprise. In a system of democratic collectivism the dilemma might or might not be mitigated; it would not be automatically resolved.

[1] See Alternative to Serfdom, pp. 88–9, 122.

Unorganized workers need protection in two great areas: wages, and human relations on the job. The effect of unions in this latter area is probably by far their most important benefit to the workers. In the last century and a quarter, there can, humanly speaking, be no doubt that real wages in this country would have risen spectacularly, with or without unions; and perhaps nearly as much as they have actually risen. Money wages might not have risen as much; but the saving to the employer would not have been allowed to remain undisturbed in his pocket. The forces that govern the level of profits would have acted from a lower level of wage costs as a base, and most of the saving would probably have been passed on to the customers, including the workers. Or, to put it the other way around, if unions, which were weak during the early part of this period, had been strong through all of it, there is no clearly convincing reason for thinking that real wages in general would now be higher than they actually are. But without unions, human rights on the job would have made far slower progress.

Insofar as unions have pushed real wages up farther than they would have risen without unions, they have probably brought more benefit than harm to the economy, and even, on balance, to employers. Their effects in the present and the future may be different, since the balance of power has shifted radically in a generation, culminating at an almost revolutionary rate in the past fifteen years. Power in either area, over wages or human relations, can go too far; no one group should have absolute power, whether employer, worker or farmer. In the area of human rights there is the question whether the protection of the worker, through his union, has in some cases encroached on the necessary power of the employer to maintain the incentives and the discipline which orderly and efficient production requires, if industry is to do its job effectively for the community as a whole. But we may put that question to one side, and concentrate on the more tangible and specific question of wages.

2. ATTITUDES OF ECONOMISTS

Here it is pertinent to inquire whether economists have kept pace with what has been happening so fast and so fatefully, in the world they study. Not that they are the last to find out what is going on; they are probably on the whole more aware of its wide import than the general run of employers or labor leaders, who are fully occupied with immediate tactics. But fifteen years is a short time to gain a true perspective on anything so far-reaching; and especially to reformulate theories that have been held for a generation or longer. Economists have been split into theorists and labor specialists. The specialist describes the bargaining process sympathetically, with its mixture of applied psychology, diplomacy, power politics, poker and an occasional dose of violent coercion. The theorist has examined imaginary "models" of equilibrium, bearing a more-than-dubious relation to the rough-and-tumble of the actual process. Each, in its own fashion, has (with recent exceptions) tended to act in ways that are warranted only on the assumption that no really radical change has taken place—that adjustments are still governed by market forces not too different from those we have traditionally trusted, and that "bargaining power" alters the action of these forces only moderately.

Until recently, it has not been fashionable with either group to call a spade a spade to the extent of speaking of "monopoly" in the sale of labor, except perhaps in exceptional cases of rather flagrant abuse. Theorists tended to acquiesce in features of the situation to which their theories did not fit. And both groups of economists seemed prevailingly to have felt that it was the duty of a "liberal" not only to give general support to organized labor, which had so long been the underdog, but to find labor's attitudes correct under almost all circumstances. This was supported by the vague and makeshift concept of "equalized bargaining power," construed to imply that, first, whatever power organized labor might get, it would still not overmatch the powers opposed to it; and that, second, so long as that was true, no serious harm was done Both ideas are questionable. The first oversimplifies the matter by conceiving the contest as solely between employers and employed, neglecting the employer's bargaining power *vis-à-vis* the customer, and the second minimizes the tendency to pass the bargaining pressure on to the customer, as the line of least resistance. This was recognized as an occasional abuse rather than as a general tendency. The situation has outgrown this makeshift treatment.

Economic theorists may suffer from a kind of split personality that goes deeper than this lag in adjusting to current reality. Traditionally, they have been "scientists" of a peculiar sort. They studied the relationships that would be fully realized in ideally free markets, and this study served two purposes. It acted as a first approximation to the study of reality, and also as a standard of what was economically sound and good—as good as possible, that is, in an imperfect world of overpopulation and limited productive power. This one theory never served both purposes perfectly, but the imperfections merely strained the tradition. Now they have shattered it. If we are going to study what exists, and also what is economically sound, we need two studies, not one: one kind of "economic law" cannot now serve both purposes.

Recently, economists seem to have been recognizing this situation, and have begun to integrate their thinking. Labor specialists in particular, have been seeking valid generalizations about the forces playing on actual wage policies and levels, in the light of their experience; and there are some in both groups who are independently asking what is economically sound. They do not assume that the actual and the good will be found identical, though they naturally cherish the hope that they may turn out to be not totally irreconcilable. The background for such realistic thinking is, of course, primarily the growth in the power and tactics of organized labor since the early years of the nineteenth century, and secondarily the special postwar stresses, with their drive toward an "inflationary spiral." There is no time to trace the steps in these developments.[1] But from it one general premise can be drawn. Labor's basic weapon, the right to strike, as now practiced, is something that does not fit economic laws of demand and supply, and raises questions that go far beyond the individual's constitutional right not to be held to specific performance of a contract for labor service. The public safety hinges on finding a solution that will not constitute "involuntary servitude," either for the worker or the rest of the community.

3. WHAT SHOULD A THEORY OF WAGES DO?

Let us start with the assumption that theory faces the twofold assignment of studying what is actual and what is economically sound. The first assignment covers the differential structure of wages and the level at which the structure stands, asking in each case what forces govern it, and to what kind of an adjustment they tend. It includes the psychology, politics and poker of wage bargaining, and also the sense of equity that enters into it: equity between different groups of workers bearing on what differentials will be tolerated and which ones will provoke counterdemands, and, to a less general extent and in a more uncertain way, equity between worker and employer, causing workers to refrain from enforcing demands which the employer clearly cannot meet. Included also are any economic factors which may set limits on the play of these bargaining forces, such as the employer's judgment of the relative value to him of different workers; or the minimum level of profit which, if impaired by wage increases, will tend to restore itself by the raising of prices. And account must be taken of the different way in which these factors may respond in booms

---

[1] The development of labor's powers and tactics has been briefly traced in Alternative to Serfdom, pp. 83–90, the postwar stresses have been summarized in the preceding lecture, and will be treated a little more fully in a study which the writer has under way for the Committee for Economic Development.

and depressions, furnishing a basis for what may be called systematic conjecture as to how they will behave in a hoped-for future of activity sustained at a high average level without major fluctuations.

The most general question is whether there are natural economic limits on what bargaining power can do in this field. If there are, they may constitute the "economic law" of wages, as distinct from the pressure politics which may govern particular and immediate adjustments. And if we can find them, they will probably put us well on the way toward filling the second main requirement and telling us what wages are economically sound. There are undoubtedly both maximum and minimum limits (neither precise nor immovable) at any well-established general level of national output (including its customary rate of increase). To these limits people's sense of what is equitable and what is attainable adjusts itself after a fashion. The chief minimum limit is probably set by the fact that there is no way to coerce workers into the kind of willing cooperation that is necessary to efficiency. If they work under a constant sense of inequity, the morale of the force suffers, and production suffers as a consequence. This is an article of our unwritten economic constitution; and it defines and prohibits "involuntary servitude" in a fashion more subtle and searching than any legal enactment could achieve.

On the other side, it is equally impossible to coerce the employer into being spontaneously enterprising and vigorous in venturesome investment; and this presumably sets a limit on the fraction of the joint income of worker and employing industry as a whole, which labor can take away from employers. Both minimum and maximum are presumably zones with fringes. If the upper fringes of the minimum overlap the lower fringes of the maximum, there may be no great harm done. Claims of right by rival groups will always add up to more than there is to divide, and any adjustment must leave some discontent. If those who make these claims do not take them too seriously, the resulting discontent need not be the kind that deadens performance. But if people's rock bottom convictions of their equitable necessities overlap and conflict, the minimum wage level may rise above the maximum. Then the economy is sick, and the principle of voluntary adjustment may be on the way out, through failure of the members to live up to the requirements of a system of group organization.

Out of many possible wage problems, I propose to concentrate on the effect of wages on employment as a natural limit, either on actual wages or on economically sound wages. It is essentially the same question that we have already asked about prices, and is about equally difficult to answer, for much the same kind of reasons. But first come some questions as to the actual behavior of wages, which furnish the setting in which their effects on employment will work themselves out.

4. THE WAGE STRUCTURE: THE ROLE OF RELATIVE WAGES

Professor Sumner H. Slichter has found evidence suggesting one normal tendency that has characterized the wage structure, at least in the past: namely, a tendency, rooted in union policy, for union wages to maintain a fairly stable differential above nonunion rates. This makes it worth while to belong to a union. It might also suggest that union rates are, after all, governed by free market forces, if the nonunion rates are the active controlling factor. But Slichter doubts whether, in the future, with the power unions now have, union wages will take their cue from the nonunion pattern. And even as to the past, there is the question whether nonunion wages were not influenced by union rates, at least as much as the other way around. Nonunion workers often do get the union rates —that is one of the union worker's grievances against the "free riders." And nonunion scales commonly show more difference than union scales, between the highest and lowest rates, even in the same establishment. All this does not add up to a convincing case that union rates are governed by free market forces.

It appears, from this and from the evidence of rates in different trades and industries, that the union sense of equity drives toward greater equality than would result from the employers' independent judgment, based on his estimate of the relative worth of different workers. And even employer policy does not pay the faster or more accurate worker the full commercial value of his superiority. That would lead to a progressive piece rate, rather than a flat one. Such an incentive is not necessary to stimulate the worker to use his talent; and there is much evidence that it tends to overstimulate many, leading to harmful overexertion. Also, it might defeat its own end by rousing labor opposition, especially if the piece rates are cut after the general pace in the shop has been speeded up.

This problem is being approached by systematic "job evaluation," presumably not with criteria that would satisfy strictly "scientific" economic standards, but far better than leaving the matter solely to the pressure politics of bargaining. That still enters in; but systematic studies have a chance to lead to an improved result. The chief effect on employment, if the workers' sense of equity leads to relative wages that are more nearly equal than the value of different workers to the employer, is presumably to make it that much harder for the slower or poorer workers to find employment or to keep it. It may be one of the factors tending to make the employer ready to welcome something appreciably short of "full employment," giving him more chance to pick and choose among his workers, and to set his minimum standards of performance higher. There are serious questions here, but we must pass them over.

If the matter of relative wages is settled somehow, it may be legitimate to take it for granted as something that maintains a good deal of stability in the structure of differential rates, general and persistent changes in the pattern being fairly gradual. In such conditions, it may further be legitimate to speak about the effects of general changes, upward or downward, in the level of the whole structure.

5. THE WAGE STRUCTURE: THE GUARANTEED ANNUAL WAGE

Another feature of the wage structure may become an active issue, if the weight of union pressure is really put behind the proposal for a guaranteed annual wage: that is, for putting all or a considerable part of the workers on more nearly the same basis as executive officials who receive an annual salary. On this large question, time permits only a few remarks. In the first place, the customary system of paying by hours or days worked or pieces turned out cannot claim to be a scientific method when it comes to distributing the risk of having inadequate work available. But neither is a system that pays as much for idle time as for work done. And a flat annual salary for every established member of the working force is a burden which could be successfully handled only by industries with highly stable demand, such as foods. Steel, construction and capital goods generally, are still exposed to the likelihood of severe fluctuations from causes beyond their individual control, to such an extent that the burden on them would be prohibitive. Instead of making for steadier jobs, the compulsory introduction of such a system might precipitate a depression starting·in these key industries and extending to others, by the familiar contagion of reduced consumer demand. At best, it does not seem appropriate to sustaining the average level of employment in prosperity and depression, and it might reduce it.

More limited forms of guarantee would avoid the extreme burden, but would add considerably to the burden already involved in unemployment insurance. Unemployment insurance is a compromise. It makes the burden (and also the total benefit) moderate, but puts the burden in the form of a tax which falls on the act of employing labor equally in good times and bad. If, as Lord Beveridge has said, adequate unemployment insurance is too heavy a financial burden unless employment can be made at least moderately stable, the same is true in greater degree of the greater burden of a guaranteed annual wage. If it were financed in the same general way, the incentive to limit employment would become too obvious; and even more so if the single employer bears the whole burden without the protection which a contributory fund affords. Once he had hired a worker and incurred this burden of paying wages whether the worker's time was used or idle, he would be under tremendous pressure to do anything possible to see that the time was used somehow. But he would be distinctly more cautious than he is now about incurring this initial liability by employing a worker who would qualify for the wage guarantee.

All that is seriously proposed at present is to encourage voluntary plans of this sort, in which the employer would be free to set limits on his liability. If he does this by limiting the number of workers who get the guarantee, most of those covered may get little or nothing more than they get now by virtue of seniority; but there would be a sharpening of the line between workers with security privileges and those without them. A more logical method would be to limit the guarantee to something less than full wages, thus giving the employees an incentive to cooperate in plans for utilizing time that would otherwise be idle. If the employer is to be under pressure to find things for his workers to do when the obvious demand falls short, he will need their willing cooperation in moving them around between types of work more freely than union restrictions now permit. This might be easier to secure if it brought the workers more pay.

But such a limited guarantee, paying less than full time wages for idle time, would bring the plan closer to an ordinary unemployment benefit. How these two would be coordinated is a sizeable problem in itself—one of many such problems that seem to be involved.

So far as concerns giving the employer an incentive to regularize employment, it is generally accepted that, while he can do a good deal to improve seasonal irregularities of the work load, he can do little, by himself, to smooth out general business cycles, under pressure of a guaranteed wage or not. Existing guarantees are not found in industries heavily exposed to cyclical fluctuations. Without wishing to be cynical, one cannot escape the thought that the plan is practicable in proportion as employment has been made substantially regular by other means; and in the same proportion the need for the guaranteed wage becomes less urgent. It would improve and complete an existing structure of stability, not initiate it. To be successful in the unstable industries, the guarantee would need to be combined with other measures stabilizing and sustaining demand for their products, so that they might find something for their workers to produce which would have enough market value to finance a major part of the guaranteed wage. Perhaps for the present the chief value of the agitation for it is to increase the pressure toward effective measures of stabilization in general.

6. THE LEVEL OF WAGES: ITS ECONOMIC LIMITS

We may start with a simple and unassailable proposition: real wages plus real profits are limited by the physical productivity of industry. Further, the relative shares of wages and profits appear to fluctuate within rather narrow limits. Precisely pertinent figures do not seem to exist, but "wages and salaries" have over a long term of years kept quite close to two thirds of the national income. This is subject to gradual long-term change, as increasing percentages of the population have come to get their incomes from wages and salaries; and the proportion would be more than two thirds in industry and large-scale trade, even after making allowance for incomes listed as salaries, but which have more of the character of a division of profits. The picture suggests a normal percentage of total product, beyond which real wages cannot easily and quickly be pushed. Why is there this consistency?

One theory would base it on the operation of the principle of "marginal productivity." Studies of the observed relation between labor, capital and output in manufacturing have been fitted into a mathematical formula which has the property that the shares assigned to labor and capital, on marginal productivity principles, would closely approximate two thirds and one third, over considerable periods of time and in widely separated economic systems.[1] As to the meaning of this observed relationship, large unsettled questions remain. If the aggregates behave in this way because individual wage payments follow marginal productivity principles, it ought to be possible to find some supporting evidence by examining the conditions of actual wage payment. But this kind of evidence points strongly to the conclusion that particular wages are not governed at all closely by marginal productivity, but are influenced by other things within fairly wide limits.

What is "marginal productivity"? The simplest and perhaps the most misleading statement is: "what an added worker will add to the product." That suggests a picture of a factory with some spare capacity, taking on an extra man, or a team of men who can put an idle machine to work turning out additional products. We may call this "short-run" marginal productivity. But it is precisely the kind of added product that cannot be the regular basis of wage payment. If it were, the men working directly on machines would get the whole product, and there would be nothing left for other necessary workers, or for management, or stockholders.[2] The kind of marginal productivity that could be a basis for the regular payment of wages grows out of a different kind of situation.

For this purpose we must think of a factory that is being modernized, and perhaps rebuilt. It is large enough to have the stand-

[1] The formula was developed by Professor Charles W. Cobb, formerly of Amherst College, in collaboration with Professor Paul H. Douglas, who made it the basis of his Presidential address to the American Economic Association in December, 1947: "Are There Laws of Production?," Amer. Econ. Rev., Mar., 1948, pp. 1–41. In the original statistical series, the data fitted an expression in which product varies with labor to the two-thirds power, multiplied by capital to the one-third power. Other data have come notably close to this pattern.

[2] For this purpose, product should be defined as "value added to materials." There are theorists who hold that prices should, in such a case, be reduced to the bare added cost of the added output, in which case the added product of the added workers would be made equal to their wages; and most plants would be incurring operating deficits most of the time. This is clearly an impracticable principle for continuous use under a system of private enterprise.

ard economies of size and, in general, is adequately equipped with capital. Possibly its techniques are so standardized that the proportions of capital and labor, at full capacity, are fixed; in that case, it is not one of the plants that play an active part in determining marginal productivity. But perhaps there are some close decisions for the engineers to make between different methods, involving more or less capital per worker, and calling for judgment as to which method would be more economical. If the judgment were close, it might be determined by the rate of wages or the cost of capital. These close marginal decisions are the ones to which the "law of diminishing returns" applies, which means that the concern can pay labor the "marginal product" which is implicit in these comparisons, and still have something left for capital, or vice versa.[1] We may call this "long-run" marginal productivity. It

[1] We might start with a hypothetical plant A, and give arbitrary values of 100 to its quotas of labor, capital and product at full capacity. Plant B, using the same amount of labor and 10 per cent more capital, might be able to turn out 3 per cent more product. If that is barely worth doing, that means that ten added units of capital have a marginal product of three, and the share of 100 units on that basis would be thirty units of product. But, by hypothesis, plant A could simply be made larger, with ten per cent more labor and ten per cent more capital, and create ten per cent more product (plant C). Comparing plant C with plant B, we find that ten units of added labor are responsible for seven units of added product. If these methods are equally economical, then labor and capital are being paid in proportion to their marginal productivities, in the ratio of seventy to thirty. If the plant just covers costs, including capital costs, then payments for labor and capital are equal to their marginal productivities, which together absorb the whole product (other shares, such as taxes, are omitted for simplicity).

This crude example is far from telling the whole story, but it illustrates the kind of comparison that is pertinent to a marginal-productivity wage theory. Obviously, once the plant is built, the outcome may differ from the expectations that governed its construction; but these expectations will have registered in the demand for capital and labor. This is subject to later revision, and the revision may be influenced by the short-run situation in which the plant is there, its cost goes on even if it stands idle, and the short-run "marginal product" of labor, up to the capacity of the plant, would absorb the whole product. That is, in terms of physical product, short-run marginal productivity of labor exceeds long-run when plant is partly idle, though at such a time the product may not be worth as many dollars as when demand is strong and plant is fully utilized. For all these reasons, the principle of marginal productivity cannot be expected to determine wages with any close approach to precision.

probably has an important underlying and limiting effect on the general wage scale producers can afford to pay. Given the costs of labor and capital, it determines the proportions in which it pays to employ them.

But this leaves many more specific questions, giving rise to doubts as to how precisely this general limiting force acts on actual wage rates. No employer knows enough about alternative methods of production to pay wages exactly on this basis. As between better and poorer workers, we have seen that differences in pay are far less than the difference in the workers' value to the employer. It would cost a good deal to measure these differences in value, and if an employer did it, and based wages on the results, he would not only be likely to get in trouble with his union, but would stimulate many of his workers to overdrive themselves and injure their health. The best workers are worth more to the employer than any extra wage they are likely to get; they get a considerable part of their extra reward in the shape of steadier and more secure employment.

Once a plant is built, and operating at a wage scale consistent with the kind of calculations the employer made when he committed himself to the venture, he will want to select the best workers he can get, but he will hire poorer ones if he needs their output to supply his customers. And if demand is sufficient, all but a small percentage of the poorest workers will be worth hiring in the short run. If wages are pushed a little higher, other things being equal, there may be a few more workers whom the concern is reluctant to hire, or it may be a little more reluctant; but it is hard to be sure that a particular wage increase will make such-and-such a worker not worth hiring. The upshot seems to be that wages register the effect of long-run marginal productivity, modified by current conditions of demand, which bring short-run marginal productivity into play. So the result is a compromise, and wages are not rigorously or uniformly determined by either kind of force.

One view is that increased wages increase productivity, and so tend to be self-sustaining. There is truth in this, but how much, and in what kinds of cases and within what limits? So far as it is a matter of the worker's own efficiency, wages may afford the enabling conditions of efficiency, or they may afford incentives. For different kinds of work, there are minimum conditions of nourishment, or of education, housing and living conditions, which are needed to enable a worker to be efficient. A localized industry may be caught in a vicious circle for lack of this minimum, and a wage increase may help to pull it out, generally in connection with other improvements. When one gets above the minimum, the enabling factors become less important and the incentives more so. These may depend less on the level of wages and more on the premiums they hold out for superior performance, both in differential pay and in the many imponderables that go to make up a high state of morale and loyalty.

Besides the worker's efficiency there is the employer's; and some keen students bank heavily on the effect of a wage increase in forcing the employer to overhaul his methods and improve them. It confronts him with a "challenge," to use Toynbee's term, and he must rise to it or suffer unpleasant consequences. This undoubtedly happens, but it seems very unsafe to go on the assumption that it will always happen, no matter how often the challenge is repeated or how large an increase in efficiency it calls for. This does, however, furnish one more reason for regarding the productivity limit on wages as a rather indefinite and moveable one.

Another reason rests on what happens if wages in various industries rise above the limit set by marginal productivity, and employers try to economize on the expensive factor of labor by introducing more labor saving equipment. This may reduce the demand for particular kinds of labor that overprices itself; but before that happens, labor must be employed in making the equipment, and the immediate net effect may be an increase in the demand for labor as a whole. It may temporarily take two to five workers to make the machine that will ultimately displace one; and if the process keeps going on, it is conceivable that the increase of employment in the labor market as a whole may keep ahead of the reduction, more or less indefinitely. This might obscure the natural check on overpricing of labor.

To sum up, the mechanisms which govern particular wage rates do not seem to behave with a precision that would explain the fairly stable proportion of the national income that goes to wages. Possibly the explanation lies rather on the other side: in forces tending to keep profits at a normal proportion of the whole, through the need of offering enough to attract capital, setting an elastic minimum below which they could not permanently fall; and the pressure of competition, which may still be strong enough to prevent profits from rising permanently much above this minimum. Back of the force of competition there may be a maximum limit of another kind, in that if profits grow at the expense of other shares, this will mean a distorted distribution of income which will reduce consumer spending, and therefore reduce the field for productive capital outlays and reduce investment spending. The reduction in total spending would then reduce profits.

This can be expressed as a formula, starting with the proposition that income (simplified for this purpose into profits plus wages) is limited to what is spent, for consumption plus capital outlays. Then the limit on profits can schematically be represented as equal to total capital outlays, plus consumer outlays out of profits, minus savings out of wages.[1] In still simpler terms, this means that profits can be maintained only to the extent that they are all spent, for consumption or capital outlays. This hypothesis as to the limit on profits, resting as it does on a distribution of income consistent with its balanced use for consumption and investment,

---

[1] This formula bears a family resemblance to a theory formulated by Mr. Jerome Levy, of New York, but is not identical with it.

is at least appropriate to the generally consistent relationship which wages and profits appear to maintain.

7. EFFECTS OF WAGES ON EMPLOYMENT

So far, we have a *prima facie* case for wages as a fairly stable fraction of the national income. If this has the qualities of a stable equilibrium, departures should tend to correct themselves. The most obvious corrective would be some form of the "law of supply and demand"; and the problem whether it works, and how, needs to be divided into two questions. (1) Will higher wages reduce the demand for labor, and so lead to unemployment if they exceed a proper level? (2) If this happens, will it result in reducing wages, and so correct itself? The two are separate questions, and the first might happen without the second, in an economy in which unions are strong, and wages are in considerable part a political issue. In this matter, economists are divided, some thinking that higher wages reduce employment and lower wages increase it, some holding that they have little or no effect, one way or the other, and some arguing that higher wages increase employment, and lower wages reduce it. Evidently, we face a difficult problem in trying to move toward resolving this disagreement.

One of the simplest answers is that, if money wages rise to a level that squeezes profits below their normal share, profits will be restored by raising prices. This may happen, and if the monetary mechanism expands sufficiently, there may be no resulting curtailment of real production and employment. If it does not expand, there may be fewer jobs. Serious as this question is, we may pass it over, and move on to the question what happens if profits do not restore themselves: that is, if the increased wages come out of reduced profits. In this case, how will employment respond?

Here we face a difficulty similar to that of general movements of prices. Wages are costs, and determine how expensive it is for the employer to hire workers. But they also furnish a large part of the buying power that is available to pay the costs. So, if one likes high wages, one can look at wages as purchasing power, and argue that higher wages increase employment. Or if one distrusts wages that seem unduly high, one can look at them as costs, and reach the opposite conclusion. The argument for raising wages to sustain employment was used in 1945-6 with considerable effect, coupled with the contention that profits were swollen and could and should absorb a large increase in wages without an increase of prices. The outcome was an increase in prices, which toned down considerably the original enthusiasm for the high wage theory, but did not resolve the dispute over the responsibility for the rising prices, or the argument that direct price controls should be re-established, if necessary, to prevent wage increases from being cancelled. The increase in prices was only partly due to increased wage costs, and centered largely in higher farm prices. Insofar as it was due to high purchasing power, the effect of high wages was complicated by a situation in which people were willing and able to spend more than the incomes they were receiving from current production.

The problem remains unsolved. If one is not an advocate of an interest, but an economist, interested mainly in finding the facts, one must recognize that wages are both costs and income. Then one has a harder problem, and must try to strike a balance between opposing forces. That is the problem I am trying to deal with here.

8. A BALANCED ANSWER TO THE PROBLEM

By way of an answer, I hope it is not too banal to suggest that it depends on how high wages were to start with, and especially whether they were above or below the range that current conditions make normal (admitting that it may be a range and not a sharp line). Wages can be so high as to reduce employment, or so low as to reduce it for a different reason; and in between there must be a range in which the level of wages is consistent with the maximum amount of employment which other conditions permit. That does not mean that the proper level of wages alone can guarantee "full employment." Obstacles of other sorts may exist. Spending may be insufficient at the existing level of prices, entry to industries and trades may be obstructed, or the differential structure of wages and prices may be such as to restrict the avenues of employment for particular groups or types of labor. All that a correct wage level can mean is that this factor in itself does not offer any avoidable obstructions.

The wage level can affect employment in two main ways. A drastic rise in wage costs can put high cost employers out of business faster than others will come in or expand to take their places. That is fairly obvious. But for less drastic movements, the net balance of effect is probably to be sought in terms of their effect on the distribution of income, and through it, on the volume of spending, by workers and recipients of profits, by individuals and business enterprises, for consumption and capital outlays. We can formulate the problem by taking total income as 100%, divided in various proportions between wages and profits, and ask what effect these various divisions have on the percentage of the total income that people will undertake to spend.

The extreme cases are fairly clear. If a general rise in wages absorbed half of total profits, they would be bought at the cost of forcing too many employers to close down, and the resulting unemployment would unquestionably reduce total payrolls in this direct fashion, aside from the less direct effect of drastically cutting down the employer's incentive to make capital outlays, which would further reduce income and employment. If one fourth of profits were absorbed, instead of half, the direct effect would be less marked, and might be offset by the effect of the redistribution of incomes, since workers, on the average, spend a larger percentage of their incomes for consumption than profit takers. To put it in figures which are not wholly conjectural, if, by a twelve per cent increase in average wage-rates, eight per cent of the initial national income were shifted from profits, where sixty-five per cent of it would have been spent for consumption, to wages where ninety per cent of it would be so spent, then an additional one fourth of the eight per cent, or two per cent more of the national income, would be spent for consumption. This is probably an optimistic estimate.[1] If hard pressed employers were exempted from the wage increase, there might be no direct reduction of employment through forcing high cost establishments to close down. But there would still be the discouraging effect on capital outlays, resulting from a rather drastic reduction of profits. If capital outlays accounted originally for fifteen per cent of the national expenditures, it seems morally certain that this change would reduce it to substantially less than thirteen per cent. This would more than offset the increase in consumer expenditures. Then total national income would shrink, and with it, real production and employment.

On the other hand, if wages were cut one third, reducing them to one half of the national income, the other half going to profits, the shift in distribution would reduce consumer spending, let us say by four per cent of the initial national income. As to the effect on capital outlays, profit margins would be wide, and funds would be easy to secure; but the question remains whether capital outlays would increase in the face of a shrinkage in consumer demand. Some modernizations might be carried through, and some new projects undertaken; but the balance of probability seems to lie on the side of a net shrinkage of capital outlays, since they depend

[1] This estimate is made on the assumption that a shift of income from profits to wages might increase the percentage spent for consumption by slightly more than an evenly distributed shift of the same amount from higher to lower income groups, as indicated by the percentages of their incomes which different income groups spend. An "evenly distributed" shift here means one by which every individual's departure from average income is reduced by the same percentage. See study by Harold Lubell, referred to above, Chap. IV, p. 111.

on demand as well as on profit margins. Then total real income and production would shrink, and with them total employment. The distribution of income that makes for maximum employment lies somewhere between the limits that have been suggested, and either a reduction or an increase of wages, beyond these limits, would reduce employment.

But these limits are wide, and as to just where the best distribution lies, no very precise answer seems possible. It appears that the effect on capital outlays is likely to be more important than the effect on consumer spending; and this is a resultant of two kinds of opposing factors, consumer demand and profit margins. Capital outlays may be roughly divided into three components. The first is the outlay required to provide the capacity to meet demand with existing methods of production. It is governed by demand, and moves with it in the long run. Fluctuations in the rate of growth of demand tend to bring intensified fluctuations in this component of capital outlays; but we can disregard these for the present, since we are looking for conditions of long-run balance.

The second component consists of increases or decreases in the margin of reserve capacity, and pioneering with new methods of production and new kinds of products. They may be called "autonomous" capital outlays.[1] They are sensitive to the general state of business optimism or pessimism, and to profit margins. They are not independent of consumer demand, but are not tied to it as closely as the first type. Conjecturally, they might be at a maximum if wages absorbed 60% or less of the total product, and might be expected to dwindle as wages rose toward 70%.

Finally, there are capital outlays that use capital to save labor, either because labor has become more expensive, or capital cheaper. They may shade into the second type, but are often clearly distinguishable. They result from high wages in particular

---

[1] The term has been used by A. H. Hansen, but he is not responsible for the above suggestion as to its precise coverage.

industries, and naturally tend to increase as wages rise, but only as long as there are still fair prospects of profits.[1] They might be at a maximum when wages absorb something between sixty five per cent and seventy per cent of the total product, but would presumably begin to dwindle before labor's share rose to seventy per cent, and beyond that, would dwindle fairly rapidly. The tentative conclusion is that something like the customary division between wages and profits is consistent with maximum capital outlays. But if something could be done to cause business to adjust itself to a narrower range of profit margins, then the best distribution might shift in favor of wages, making it economically sound to pay higher wages, and bringing us nearer to the high consumption type of economy which was earlier indicated as affording an ideal balance which would be more stable than we have experienced in the past. A good deal may hinge on whether business succeeds in making this adjustment. Of course it will not if it does not try.

Are there any indications as to whether the actual distribution is above the best level, or below it, or in a range in which a small change in wages would make little or no difference to employment? One answer says that it must be above, since if it were below, the level of production and employment would be in unstable equilibrium. An increase of wages would increase the demand for labor, and tend to a further rise in wages, and a reduction would have the reverse effect. This answer would be persuasive if wage rates were sensitively responsive to changes in the demand for labor; but under present conditions they are not, especially in a downward direction. Not only union bargaining power, but the general feel-

[1] The point has been made that the effect might be neutralized if high wages in the capital producing industries increased the costs of capital equipment by as much as labor-costs had increased, in which case "labor saving machinery" would be no more economical than before, unless interest rates were reduced. In general, increased wages do not appear to have raised the costs of mechanical equipment enough to neutralize the power of increased mechanization to economize expensive labor. Mechanization in the capital producing industries themselves would appear to have prevented the prices of such equipment from rising as much as wages have risen. Increased scale of production also tends to make increased mechanization more economical.

ing of workers, employers and the public, acts as a powerful obstacle to a reduction of wages when demand shrinks. And the evidence of business fluctuations is that the economy *is* in an unstable equilibrium, between fairly wide limits which seem to be set largely by other factors than changes in wage rates. So the fact that it does not go beyond these rather indefinite limits does not furnish convincing evidence that we are in the zone in which increased wages reduce employment.

One reason for thinking we are in this zone arises from the inherent tendency of collective bargaining, with unions at their present strength, to push wages upward until they reach some fairly compelling limit. This may be conceded as a fact; but it still leaves open the question whether the nature of the limit is a reduction of employment or some other combination of forces. The argument seems to presuppose that the bargaining power of unions is stronger than that of employers. Superficially, the experience since the war points in that direction; but this has been a time of extra-strong demand, when employers were not forced to use to the utmost their bargaining power against labor, because they could more easily use it in the direction of the customer. The limit on real wage increases consisted mainly in the rise of prices, which proves nothing for our present purpose. It merely means that under these conditions a rise in money wages would not bring about a rise in real wages; hence it fails to prove what the effect of a rise in real wages would have been. Employers were able to protect their margins without having to face the test whether higher real wages would have meant fewer jobs.

A more genuine test comes when employers, being unable or unwilling to raise prices, turn to resisting wage demands more stubbornly, and testing their bargaining power in this direction. Then one of three things may happen. The employers may be able to protect their necessary margins by checking wage increases before they reach the level that would mean fewer jobs, or they may check them only after they have reached this level, or they may fail to check them, in which case employment may shrink, either because employers' margins have been reduced or because higher prices, in a less buoyant market than that of 1946–7, have curtailed demand. The first outcome would prove nothing; the other two would indicate that we are in the zone in which higher wages do mean fewer jobs. But the answer would be very difficult to prove, even if employment were to shrink, because there are other things that might bring this about, besides high wages. Prospects are not bright for reaching agreement as to whether employers have succeeded in protecting profit margins that are higher than are needed to induce them to furnish a maximum number of jobs.

Perhaps the strongest indications come from comparing the rate of increase in productivity, which sets the ultimate limit, with the rate to which union organization appears to be geared, in the light of union politics and the pressure it puts on leaders to produce gains that will not fall too far short of promises and will keep the membership from becoming so dissatisfied as to lead to revolt. Productivity sets a limit at an annual average gain of not more than three per cent—probably less, in the long run. And union organization is plainly geared to substantially larger gains than this. Leaders may recognize the economic limits more clearly than the rank and file; but they also recognize that a single union always has a chance to gain more than the average; or it can fall behind the more aggressive ones and lose ground relatively.

Insofar as there is a tendency to maintain something like the customary scale of differentials, it seems to work in a setting in which particular unions are continually disturbing it by making individual gains, and those who feel themselves disadvantaged take action to restore their relative standing, the adjustments that are sought being always upward. Add the fact that the employer's need for good labor relations is increasing, and may be becoming more urgent than his need of the good will of his customers. This all adds up to a situation in which either money wages rise faster than productivity permits real wages to rise, or in which it will be hard to avoid serious trouble for leaders, employers and the public. Perhaps it will be hard to avoid trouble, whatever wages do. This picture seems on the whole to afford the strongest reason for believing that wages tend to push past all the less rigorous limits which oppose their indefinite increase, and to rise into the zone in which further increase means reduced employment.

9. WHICH IS MORE SERIOUS, TOO HIGH WAGES OR TOO LOW?

Within the margin of uncertainty, the instinct of our society is to give the benefit of the doubt to higher wages; and this instinct is almost certainly sound. In times past, wages have lagged behind profits, and a more rapid increase would probably have made for a healthier society. In England, at the opening of the nineteenth century, a great burst of industrial expansion was probably furthered by a rise in prices, with wages lagging behind, thus reducing real wages and the wage cost of producing manufactured goods. But British industry in this period was different from American industry of today in one vital respect: it was not dependent for its market on selling its goods to its own wage earners—not to anything remotely approaching the extent to which American industry is so dependent today. It could prosper while they were impoverished; that road to prosperity would be suicide for present American mass-production industry.

If economic forces leave wages a little too low, there may be no dependable automatic corrective. On the other hand, if they go a little too high, industry can generally correct the balance by a moderate rise in prices; it has that safety valve available. We have already suggested that if this rise in prices does not go beyond two per cent a year, it is not a serious matter. Even if it goes beyond this for a year or two, no great harm is done. But in that case the rise in prices needs to be taken as a warning of something wrong, and as affording a breathing space in which to do something about it. Otherwise, it would become serious.

So, though it may be justifiable to give rising wages the benefit of any doubt that may exist, there is no excuse for being negligent in the task of narrowing the margin of doubt, and clarifying the issues as much as the stubborn nature of the problem permits. At present, it is anything but safe to assume that all disputes should be resolved in favor of increased wages. For one thing, if that were done in practice, it would be too likely to mean more gains for the workers who are most strongly organized, and who are already better paid than the average; while those most in need of increases lagged behind. Further, if too high wages do lead to unemployment at some future time, this will not lead to an automatic corrective, but rather to persistent argument that the true source of the trouble is that wages are too low to furnish sufficient purchasing power. It is important to gain clarity before we have to meet this situation, if it is at all possible.

10. A THEORY OF SOUND WAGES

In gaining this needed clarity, one of the most crucial elements is a theory of economically sound wage adjustment, formulated in terms that might actually serve as guides to negotiators; mediators and arbitrators. It needs to be capable of being translated into dollar figures (though of course only approximately). And it needs to include both an ideal or correct standard, and an estimate of the degree of departure from this ideal which the economy can tolerate without too serious damage. It could then serve to create at least a prima-facie case against gross departures. It is distinct from the theory of what governs actual wages, but can have a two-way relation to it. The actual forces may be of a character calculated to depart from the ideal in one direction or another; and this may afford contributory evidence as to where the ideal standard lies. And the economically correct standard may come to have an increasing effect on actual wage adjustments.

Under present conditions, the factors determining actual adjustments have almost—not quite—ceased to be economic, and their relation to standards of economic correctness is tenuous and doubtful. If the two are to come together again, it must be in an atmosphere in which negotiators are not simply seeking the greatest immediate gains which their organized power permits, but are concerned with what is soundly attainable, and are ready to construe this in the light of an adjustment that will stand the test of fairness, in the light of the necessities of the opposite party and of equity toward other members of the economy. In the final lecture, we shall have something to say about ways in which this attitude may be approached. For the present, we may assume it, and ask what kind of wages it requires.

First, increased average real wages for the whole economy depend on increased average productivity. As a first approximation and a point of departure, it may be assumed that they should increase at the same rate that productivity increases, maintaining their customary proportion to the whole product. This customary proportion is not sacred or immutable, and in the long run some moderate increase in labor's share may be possible and would be desirable, to the extent that business can adjust its own sound requirements to such a change; but no great and sudden change is practicable, so long as the economy remains mainly on a basis of private enterprise. To implement this standard, the first requirement is a statistical measure of the rate of increase in average productivity which is pertinent and satisfactory for this purpose. The second is a similar statistical measure, going as far back in time as practicable, of the proportions in which product is divided between wages and profits. For this primary purpose, a fairly crude measure might be sufficient, though for other purposes, the inquiry would have to go farther, and would encounter some difficult questions.

Second, some consideration should be given to the question whether actual current profits are more or less than customary, in the light of current economic conditions, and whether they constitute a fair and adequate share, and not substantially more or less, either in particular industries or in the economy as a whole. For this purpose, irrelevant items would need to be eliminated from both sides of the balance: for instance, the higher executives' salaries should be segregated and not lumped under "wages and salaries." The treatment of profit-sharing plans might raise some difficult problems; and some part of the highest executives' salaries might also be judged to be in effect a division of profits. Here the first step would naturally be an estimate of how much these doubtful items amount to and how fast, if at all, their relative importance is changing. Such an estimate might indicate that they do not disturb the over-all picture enough to be a substantial factor in actual wage determinations. On the profit side, unusual inventory profits should probably be eliminated. There will undoubtedly be some unavoidable disagreement as to the adequacy of deductions for various kinds of reserves; but here again a survey might show that changes from the customary allocations have not introduced a large disturbing element into the total picture.

The analysis would properly include the past behavior of the shares in the product during business fluctuations; and some consideration of probable normal reactions in case the country succeeds in its present efforts to maintain a higher and more stable level of production and employment in the future than it has maintained in the past. But the basic thing would be an agreement, at least "in principle," on a measure of actual profits that would be meaningful for the purpose in hand; and the figures would need to be made available in wage cases. This will be far from easy, but it should not be impossible.

To the extent that single wage adjustments affect the wage structure of an entire industry, the pertinent figures need to include an industry wide picture of the structure of profits and losses, not merely the figures for the particular employer or employers whose wages may be under negotiation. If one enterprise is more profitable than others in its industry, its superior "ability to pay" wages is not a proper basis for a wage increase unless the other employers and workers in the industry are prepared to accept the existence of a differential for this employer. The presentation of the facts would presumably have to be done in ways that would not identify particular concerns which are not parties to the negotiations. Indeed, if there is full acceptance of the principle of industry profits rather than single firm profits, no firms need be identified except where single large firms have identifiable characteristics which could not be concealed without stultifying the survey. Even industry-wide aggregates of profits and losses would mean something useful. Such a survey would not settle all questions of equity; but with the actual figures available, issues of equity should at least be clarified.

Third, individual industries' hourly wage scales should, over, let us say, a ten-year period, rise as much as the average increase in man-hour productivity for the whole economy, and not more, except as may be necessary to rectify inequities between trades and industries. This leaves room for an upward bias, since the adjustments of inequities would be prevailingly upward; and this would presumably cause the total wage structure to exceed the original average standard; but it should be possible to keep this excess within the bounds of tolerable price inflation, already discussed. With experience, it should be possible to do better than this, by learning how much this upward bias amounts to, and making some allowance for it in setting the original over-all yearly rate of increase which is taken as a point of departure.

If one industry has led in improvements or is otherwise in a position to pay more than the average increase in productivity, it may equitably share a part of the excess gain with its workers; but not generally more than average productivity could catch up with in a few years. Gains above this amount should be shared between increased profits and reduced prices, with the general presumption that within a few years competition would hand over to the customers substantially the whole gain from any single improvement. Thus neither the employers nor the workers in this industry would become intrenched in a permanently favored position. This is substantially what competition would be expected to do, if it were working in fair and unrestricted fashion.

If one industry has been unable to increase productivity as much as the average, its workers are still entitled to wages bearing a relation to other wages which fairly represents the quality and requirements of the work they do, rising in general with the average rise in productivity in the whole economy. Then prices in these industries would have to rise, offsetting the reduction of prices in industries which have increased productivity more than the average. If the industry is a declining one, and the market will not stand a rise in prices without serious reduction in output and employment, the resulting hardship may be shared between subnormal profits and subnormal wages, where it is to the workers' interest to bear a share of the hardship, as the alternative to an unduly sharp shrinkage in employment.

Industries in which demand is expanding rapidly may offer wage premiums to attract an increasing labor-force. But, as in the case of industries that lead in improvements, the premium should not be more than the average gain in productivity can make up in a few years; otherwise the expansion premium is likely to harden into a permanent wage differential, after the need for rapid expansion is over and the differential has become simply an inequitable advantage, which workers in other industries will be striving to rectify.

Industries exposed to severe rivalry from substitute products, especially new substitutes, may be unable to pay as much as these principles call for. In such hard pressed industries it is probably in the interest of the workers to make some wage concessions as the lesser evil, the alternative being a skimping of capital outlays, including maintenance, possible bankruptcy of some employers, and reduced employment. The general principle of concessions to hard pressed employers has been followed to some extent in the garment trades, coupled with assistance in maintaining standards of productivity.

This proposed principle of wage determination has one potential advantage, which might or might not be realized, and one potential weakness, which might or might not be avoided. The advantage lies in giving definiteness to the dependence of wages on productivity, and thus enlisting the interest of labor on the side of increasing productivity rather than restricting it. But this is contingent on freeing labor from the fear that increased productivity will mean fewer jobs. So success on the wage front does not stand alone, but is bound up with the other features of a successful program for maintaining total demand.

The weakness of the proposed wage principle lies in the fact that money wages would automatically rise with a rising price level. As a result, if the initial adjustment contained an inflationary bias, this might be perpetuated in the form of the familiar wage-price spiral. A good deal would depend on starting the system in a period in which the price structure was fairly stabilized. If this were done, the drive for increased wages would cease to be a further serious inflationary factor, since the chief danger on this score results from wages which increase more than the over-all increase in productivity.

What has been done here is simply to codify, as definitely as possible, the kind of long-run determinations that healthy competition would approximate, minus cyclical ups and downs of wages in response to short-run shifts of supply and demand. If it were accepted in principle, and implemented in the ways suggested, there should be a fighting chance of making such a standard approximately effective in practice. In the next and final lecture, we shall look at some of the conditions on which the acceptance of such a standard depends.

CHANGING BALANCES: UNCOMMON RE-QUIREMENTS FOR THE COMMON MAN

1. THE BALANCE OF MOTIVES AND FORCES IN COLLECTIVE BARGAINING

In the preceding lecture we faced the fact that labor relations have become the field of action of a new array of powers, which so far do not seem to have found their way to any stable balance. Wages no longer need obey the kind of laws which custom and economic doctrine have approved as sound; not unless the political and quasi-political powers that rule these matters should decide that these are good laws to follow. If they should so decide, wages might be fixed on the principles we have been examining and trying to formulate; but we have still to explore what ground there is for hoping that the conflicting parties might allow that much statesmanship to creep· into their bargaining attitudes.

So·far, the story of the labor movement has started with groups who did not have the power to get what they wanted, and has been concerned with the means by which they might gain that power. Now so many of them have gained so much of it that the great question is no longer how to get power, but how to restrain its use without "regimentation": how to induce groups that have power to use it only to get such things as all might have on the same terms. That is an exacting standard to set; but it is the standard that is implicit in a society that is both free and democratic, and unless ordinary Americans can rise to it in fair degree, democracy will not work in any economic system. The only reason why that fact did not make itself evident long ago is that it is only recently that organized power has been so widely distributed.

The unfavorable factors are numerous and obvious, some applying to labor, some to employers, some to both. Some are rooted in the human and technical factors that limit the size of the pie that is to be divided, and the competitive factors that further limit one employer's sector of the pie. Some stem from the self-centered qualities of human nature, reinforced by many generations of a too individualistic philosophy, and accentuated by a deal of what can only be described as natural cussedness. And some are perversions of the process we call "politics." One hopes they are the perversions of immaturity, and that we may ultimately outgrow the worst of them, but they are stubborn and deep-rooted.

The past has left both sides with plenty of grievances, real or cultivated; and the resulting resentment nourishes a brand of politics too prone to quarrel over the past, at the risk of losing the future. The public or semipublic character of industrial disputes leads both sides to take too rigid positions too publicly, often attaching a spurious finality to terms more favorable than they actually expect to secure—terms originally announced for bargaining effect. Since these positions are irreconcilable, any settlement necessarily leaves one side or both partially or wholly defeated in what it has taught itself to think, or to claim, are its rights and just expectations, and confronted with a need of "saving face," which may lead to including features in the settlement which have no other justification. Any possible settlement is likely to be denounced by one side or both as unfair.

On labor's side, there is the union's need to gain and hold its members, first by rousing ambition for gains which can be secured only by organization, and then by making gains for which it can claim credit. This need on the part of the union becomes identified with the leader's need to bring home some bacon whenever a contract is renegotiated, whether or not the bacon exists in the shape of a surplus which can be divided. If some other union has gotten more, he feels he has lost ground, especially if it is a rival union in his own trade or industry, which might take his members away from him. If one union gets more than its share of the pie, the loss falls mainly on others, and labor's part of the loss falls mainly on other workers. If one union refrains while others get more than their share, it loses with no compensating gain. Competition between national unions does not, like competition of producers for customers, tend to reduce prices, but to raise them. The unions compete in selling their bargaining services to the workers, and the service consists in extracting more from the employer.

In this "hard-boiled" game, the prudent employer must beware of offering at the start all he is willing to concede. Even if he wants to give his workers that much, it is generally a mistake to make them a voluntary present of it, and union leaders would not want him to, for the simple reason that it would deprive them of the credit of extracting it from him. It is to be hoped that this factor will diminish in importance as unions gain in maturity and security. In its more extreme forms it is a product of the early, fighting stage of union development. And it is a serious obstacle to progress toward a stage in which bargaining might become a process in which each side might be seeking a settlement that would be fair to both, and would stand valid tests of equity and economic soundness for the community as a whole.

Another form of this same bedevilment occurs when the leader cultivates hostility toward the employer on the part of the membership, though his personal attitude when dealing with the management is entirely cooperative. This serves two purposes. In the leader's dealings with the employer, the members' serve as the absent Jorkins, enabling him to assume a cooperative attitude and still drive a hard bargain. And in his dealings with his own members, the leader's interest lies in making the members feel that they need him to protect their rights. This maneuver probably becomes such an integral and ingrained part of the labor leader's set of attitudes that he would be surprised and indignant to be told that it is a form of hypocrisy and double-dealing, poisoning the necessary basis of tolerable relations. It is merely an example of one of the oldest of political devices: that of building up an enemy, real or fictitious, against whom the politician promises to protect the people. It becomes harmful when the enemy thus built up is one with whom constructive and co-operative dealings are a necessity, and the seriousness increases with the importance of these dealings. A William Hale Thompson, promising Chicago's voters to "bust King George in the snoot," was never a harmless political curiosity; the corresponding international attitude today is an intolerable attack on one of the few remaining strongholds of international friendship and collaboration, in a world where this has become the one indispensable safeguard against catastrophe.

As for the employer, all he needs to make him hard to deal with is to be over impressed with his traditional rights, stemming from ideas of absolute ownership, under which he may do what he will with his own as a strictly private affair. When he yields, as nowadays he must, to the principle of unionism, including the right of the outside organizer to enter his private preserves, he may still do it under a sense of injustice, and be reluctant to acquiesce in the inevitable tactics of organization. They are inevitable, even though shot through with demagoguery, because they include, interwoven with their abuses, things which are necessary to the life and growth of the socially necessary institution of unionism.

So much for the unfavorable factors; what of the favorable ones? If it be true, as Bentham was driven to believe, that men organized in groups are incurably selfish, is there a remedy in making the selfishness more intelligent and farsighted? At the risk of being dogmatic, I will say, not unless something else is added to the mixture. I have elsewhere argued that sheer calculating intelligence does not prevent conflict, but rather leads to invading one another's rights and interests, up to the point where the gain does not seem worth the "calculated risk" of provoking the other side to violent reaction.[1] But if calculated risks of conflict are regularly taken, it is only a matter of time before the risk materializes and conflict breaks out. Someone, sometime, is sure to miscalculate. Still less can such calculation be expected to lead opposing groups to adopt a self-denying standard that would define rights and put an end to rivalry for relative and invidious gains. Instead self-interest leads to the political perversions we have just been looking at; and the kind of self-interest that works in this way is animated by intelligence well above the average.

One of the keys to the way in which group self-interest works is the size and character of the group. What range of interests does it represent? In general, we rely on two kinds of groups to make group interest safe for the community: the group small enough to be checked by the competition of other similar groups, selling the same thing to the same ultimate buyer; and the group large enough and comprehensive enough to include within itself a fair representation of the opposing interests in the case. The obvious examples are the competing business enterprise on the one side, and government on the other. In between lies the group that includes all the sellers of one thing in one market: in other words, the group that has a monopoly position, and can promote its group interest by raising the price of what it has to sell, in proverbial monopoly fashion. It is plain that collective bargaining with national unions is an example of this intermediate grade of grouping, precisely the kind that makes the trouble. A logical way out might lead in one of two directions: toward breaking up unions in a way that would restore competition in the labor market, or developing them into such comprehensive groups that they would include effective representation of the interests that have to pay the costs of an exploitively monopolistic policy on the part of the workers in any one industry or trade. The first course

[1] See Alternative to Serfdom, pp. 136–8.

is out of the question; the second has some possibilities, though it is not an easy and automatic formula.

To restore competition by smashing unions, history would have to reverse itself in a way history seldom does; and it would mean the destruction of a social unit that has become indispensable. Any serious attempt to do this would be an invitation to civil war. There appears to be only one thing that would smash American unions: namely, if this country were to pass under a totalitarian system, either fascist or soviet. Under either, one of the first moves would be to subjugate unions, reducing them to obedient state agencies. Short of this, national unions might conceivably be broken up into units coextensive with the employing business unit and having some of its competitive incentive to enlarge its volume of sales, and so increase employment for the members of the individual union. This also seems out of the question. So long as our government retains its present character, the most it will do to unions is to trim off some exaggerated powers—powers which depend on positive legal protection. The Taft-Hartley Act is an experiment of this sort, which will presumably be altered by experience, but contains (among other things) some protections for union members which they (as distinct from leaders) should be slow to want to throw away.

But it is significant that many students are looking in the opposite direction. It is sometimes suggested that the way to induce unions to behave responsibly is to let them gain more nearly absolute power, power so great that whatever happens is their doing, and they not only take the credit but bear the blame, if any. It is not always clear whether those who hold this position are looking toward a full-fledged system of guild socialism, or merely to a system in which wages are fixed at whatever rates unions decide to insist on, and employers have lost all power of effective resistance. In either case, the idea that completely unrestricted power tends to develop responsibility in its use, appears to be a fundamental fallacy. Responsibility goes with power, not when the power is unrestricted, but when it is under the scrutiny of some independent entity with power to do something about it.

Increasing the power of national unions which are already strong would not make for greater responsibility in any dependable fashion. What does have a natural and calculable tendency in this direction is the exercise of influence by the great federations on the policies of their constituent bodies. These federations are comprehensive enough so that, when one constituent union makes a gain that will mean a rise in prices, the bulk of the federation's members are affected in their capacity as consumers who do not want prices to rise. It is not at all out of the question that the influence of a great federation might be thrown in favor of the kind of wage standard we have just been considering; though this might have to wait for industrial relations to make some further progress toward maturity, with a dwindling of the emphasis on wage issues and a compensating increase in the attention paid to other phases of the relation of a worker to his job, to his superiors and to his fellow workers. Otherwise, unions and their leaders would be surrendering too much of their essential reason for existence.

Another thing that might make for a more two-sided attitude is the development by unions of activities—for example, banking or cooperative distribution—in which the union becomes itself an employer. Some of the employees of unions are members of other unions—for example, unions of office workers. Others are undoubtedly unorganized, and some are expected to accept financial sacrifices for the cause of unionism. One wonders what would happen if there should come into existence an international union of the employees of labor unions: necessarily an industrial union, possibly organized within John L. Lewis' protean Local 50. There is no more practical force working for equity than a situation in which roles are reversed, regularly and frequently, so that rules may have a chance to work both ways, as a matter of familiar everyday experience. One quaint jurisdictional question might arise: to what union should the employees of the employees' union belong? That might be referred to the same authority—if it can be found—which had to deal with the alleged jurisdictional dispute (possibly apocryphal) between the roofers and siders over the work on Quonset huts. Seriously, however, the growth of union activities in which the union plays the role of employer seems bound to be favorable to the development of wage standards marked by two-sided equity.

Another thing that might work in the same direction, in a way only slightly different, is the growth of labor representation in business or industry. This is sound in principle, but presents plenty of practical problems and one substantial danger. It is clearly not appropriate except to the extent that labor wants it, and wants the responsibilities that go with it. Granting this, it is something that can probably best be worked up to, experimentally. At the early stages, workers' representatives would presumably cooperate with the lower grades of supervisory officials, but would still be responsible to the higher levels of management; and any policy recommendations that might result would be subject to the approval of management. A major step would be involved if and when representatives of labor took a place on boards of directors, to which the higher management is itself responsible. The danger is that if decisions on output and price are participated in by representatives of a national union, which is also represented in the councils of competing enterprises, the result may be contrary to antitrust policy, promoting a situation in which workers and employers might compose their differences upward, and charge the bill to the customer.

Would greater democracy in unions help? For the purpose in hand, this is a weak reliance. If a monopolistic group represents its members' interests more perfectly, that may make it more monopolistic in its policies, not less. Students of the problem are looking rather in the opposite direction, to strengthening the position of leaders in wage policy, considering that they take a longer and more comprehensive view in such matters than do the rank and file. This need not mean increasing the arbitrary authority of the leaders in all matters; it could well go along with the imposing of checks on their authority to discipline their members. Indeed, where good standing in a union is a necessary condition of holding one's job, the power to deprive a worker of such standing becomes something that should be exercised only for serious and well-defined offenses, and subject to some kind of quasi-judicial process to protect the worker's rights. Unions have limited the employer's arbitrary power of discharge, and this is justifiable in principle, so long as it is not abused to undermine the essentials of shop discipline. Limitations on the union's own power of arbitrary discharge are equally called for, on the same principle.

Taking unions and employers as they stand, one favorable factor is the gradual tendency to develop a mature bargaining attitude. This means mutual willingness to stop short of injuring the system, and realization that each party should respect the genuine necessities of the other party's position—the things he must have, in order to do his job successfully for the ultimate mutual benefit of both. That is one way of defining each party's "natural rights." The employer needs to be financially solvent, if he is to go on offering ample and expanding employment. The union has to make a showing of benefits gained, and the leader, on behalf of the union, has to make a showing that will not be too unsatisfactory to his members. Employers who have a mature bargaining attitude are willing to give him the chance to make such a record, especially if his general attitude seems fair.

In one case, the union negotiators made an oversight in a proposal, which was too much to the employer's interest, and would have gotten them into trouble with their members, and the employer called their attention to it and gave them a chance to expunge it from the record. Later in the same negotiation, they reciprocated when the employer made a similar slip. Perhaps it is more common to find one side wanting to save the other side from itself by dissuading them from demands that are too grasping and could not soundly be granted. That, for some reason, is not so easy, but it may gradually become less difficult, with progress toward more specific definition of the genuine needs of each side in the case.

If the negotiators themselves have not achieved the necessary maturity of attitude, a second line of defense is the fine art of mediation, and a third is "fact finding"—that brand of arbitration without formal power which is so prevalent today. The key to both consists largely of feeling out the needs of the parties, which are often well concealed behind their demands and arguments, and finding a settlement that will reconcile them. Dexter M. Keezer, in an enlightening article on the War Labor Board, describes how representatives of one side on a tripartite board, though acting as special pleaders for their side, can drop hints which, with the aid of continuous contact, are useful to their associates in uncovering the basis for such a reconciliation.[1]

Another method, not wholly consistent with the ends of mediation, is the practice of treating leading cases as setting "patterns," and arguing the pattern case before the bar of public opinion. The "pattern" is never closely followed—indeed, it may appear to have almost vanished when the statistical record is canvassed. And the level of argument used in public statements may sometimes be discouraging to one's confidence in democratic processes; but at least it recognizes the community as an umpire.

All of these variegated elements have one thing in common. They add up to a movement in the direction of an attitude increasingly hospitable to the development of agreed codes, more specific than the broad generalities which past efforts in this direction have succeeded in producing. They afford an increasing chance to implement the growing idea that adjustments should be

---

[1] See Dexter M. Keezer, "The National War Labor Board," Amer. Econ. Rev., June, 1946, pp. 233–257.

capable of being based on facts and reason, not on a mere test of strength. The codes would express the minimum rights of the parties, and would need to be flexible enough to leave room for evolution. They would deal with many matters. The tentative wage code which was suggested in the preceding lecture, is merely a sample of one kind of goal toward which this kind of evolution might be directed.

2. CHANGING BALANCES IN OTHER AREAS

So much for the changing balance in the realm of collective bargaining. In other areas of life, some of the changes are even more disturbing. In the international sphere, the world is struggling to bring order, necessarily a new order, out of a chaos that threatens everything we have thought of as progress since the beginning of the supposedly enlightened nineteenth century. The international balance of power has been revolutionized: in fact, the present power structure may be inconsistent with balance as the nineteenth-century concept of "balance of power" envisaged it. And national rivalry is now interwoven with a struggle between economic and social systems. Revolutionized also is the military balance between offense and defense, offense being strengthened and defense relatively weakened, to an extent which we must hope never to learn by experience. The economic balance between regions of the world has been upset. Germany is prostrate and Britain impoverished, trade betweeen eastern and western Europe is hampered, while shifts in population and resources leave some areas more dependent on foreign trade than ever before. And in struggling to resolve these manifold disturbances, the world is also struggling to establish a new balance between sovereign nationalisms and international organization and action.

In this country, there are changing balances between regions, between urban, suburban and rural areas and populations, and between occupations. It is hard to realize that the prevalent type was once the farmer; now farmers account for only fifteen per cent of the gainfully employed, and the prevalent type is the urban employee. Farming, once the economic backbone of the country, is on a pension: sometimes justified partly by the service the farm renders in raising children to replenish the less prolific urban centers. Railroads were once a source of great fortunes; now they are in difficulties, and so is bituminous coal. We have made our great gains in productiveness in the mass production of material things, with mechanical power, industrial chemistry and electronics succeeding one another in the limelight. Manufacturing processes convert materials into more valuable forms with amazing economy, and these triumphs reduce the amount of room that is left for further gains from the same source. We already spend a diminishing percentage of our total productive energy on it, and an increasing percentage on getting the materials, distributing the product, and on services. This last seems to be true, despite the fact that domestic service in the home is diminishing, and much of it has, in effect, moved into the factories that make mechanical household equipment. It would appear that the opportunities for mass-production economies have not been so great in the fields of distribution and direct services, and this is likely to continue to be true.

This seems particularly true of services of recreation, education and health, and other professional services, all of which will be increasingly important parts of our future economy. Increases in the effectiveness of effort in these directions will be measured—or should be—in terms of improved quality of service, rather than increased quantity per hour of time spent by the teacher, the doctor or the public servant. The upshot is that it is not safe to count too absolutely on being able to maintain that three per cent per year increase in average productivity per man-hour, which we took as a point of departure in estimating a sound rate of increase in real wages.

With all this goes a changing economic balance between classes. In this country, this has meant strides toward greater equality of

disposable incomes (incomes after taxes). The educational privileges of veterans have given an enormous impetus to education of
college and university grade: an impetus which may go a long
way and have lasting effects on the educational system. Another
great educational frontier is that of adult education, of which
more later. On the economic side, the changing balance is, at least
temporarily, lowering the real incomes of a considerable section
of the old "middle class"—those not engaged in business—and
is developing a new middle class in the upper ranks of "labor";
with the income that goes with middle-class status, and the educational, cultural and recreational opportunities that go with higher
income and shorter hours. This amounts to a change in the
balance between work and leisure: the culmination of changes that
have been going on at an accelerated pace for over a century. It
is likely to do something to the balance between consumption,
saving and capital outlays, though precisely what it will do remains
to be seen when temporary postwar reactions have spent their
force. At any rate, this balance is becoming a conscious problem
and a subject for deliberate policy.

There is a changing balance between government and business,
in two ways. The most obvious one is a great increase in the
activities of formal government. Less obvious, but hardly less important, are the changes outside of formal government whereby
essentially political, juridical or coercive ways of deciding things
have increased enormously at the expense of what we used to think
of as economic ways. We have been looking at some outstanding
examples of this, in connection with collective bargaining. Private
organizations, of business, labor and agriculture, are developing a
political and governmental character, making collective decisions
dealing with rights, wrongs and coercive remedies; and therefore
they are no longer fully private, but are affected with a public
interest, and in many cases can fairly be called forms of unofficial
government.

Inside formal government there are changing balances between executive, legislative and judicial power, some of which are loaded with importance for the future character of our political organization. The Supreme Court, once accused of indulging in judicial legislation, is now characteristically abstaining from substituting its judgment for that of Congress; and it accords much the same respect to the decisions of the administrative-legislative-judicial agencies which Congress sets up. Congress has so much power that it is forced to delegate a great deal of it; and not only the detail of execution, but to a large extent the formation of policy, subject to Congress' power to overrule a policy it does not like. And we have seen that when it comes to a policy of restraining business fluctuations by watching current conditions and taking appropriate action, the power to act has to rest with the executive, if it is to be prompt enough to be effective. It must be governed by mechanical formulas or must leave a great deal to executive discretion. Such increases in executive power appear inevitable, and, so far as one can see, permanent.

Within the economy, there are changing balances of many sorts. One results from the increasing emphasis on security, at the expense of old-fashioned reliance on free bargaining under conditions of unmitigated competition. This is obvious in the field of labor, where social security puts a floor under the competitive struggle, while unionism directly limits competition, with the formal approval of the community. It is equally obvious in. the field of agriculture, and there are other industries in which efforts are being made to protect them from the damaging effects of unrestricted competition.

More broadly, there has long been a race between technical innovation and social adaptation, in which technical innovation has unexpected social impacts, and the social adjustments that are needed to take care of these impacts proverbially lag behind the need. Radio, atom splitting and electronics generally, are moving this old contest into new areas, and will create new problems for the coming generation. Another phase of this is the contest be-

tween community planning and individual choice; another is the
contest between self-interest, group interest and the interest
of the community. Over all of this is the major contest between
authority and freedom, in which many old freedoms have had to
give way before the encroachments of authority, until there is
genuine ground for the fear that the requirements of the modern
world are inconsistent with those of a free society, at least as we
have known it in the past. The use of authority is certainly increasing in the material realm, partly for reasons unavoidably bound
up with mass production and applied science. But we have it in
our power to set limits on the lengths to which this will go. If we
want freedom, and meet the necessary conditions, we can maintain
the essentials of it. But we must want it enough to exercise it
responsibly, otherwise it will be displaced, whether we want this
to happen or not. It is for us to understand this, to learn what
responsible exercise of freedom means, and to put it in practice.

In the field of beliefs, morals and personal conduct, the trend
is certainly toward more freedom and away from the rule of
authority, to an extent that would have shocked and alarmed a
previous generation, and is probably a new thing in the world. The
present move toward restricting organized communism does not
belie this, but on the whole confirms it. What is being restricted
is not freedom to believe in any economic system, and to work to
convert others to that belief, but an organized movement which
would use freedom only long enough to gain the power to suppress
it by force. We are defending the freedom of the American people
to have the system that comes nearest representing their collective
desires and convictions.

In the conflict between the authority of religious belief and
the freedom of scientific skepticism, religious authority has been
consistently retreating from areas in which it clashes with scientific
evidence. But this contest, which science is winning, is dangerously liable to be confused with another conflict, from which it
needs to be kept distinct. There is a conflict between faith as such

and indiscriminate skepticism which discredits all faiths and all values. If this is settled in favor of indiscriminate skepticism, humanity may well be doomed, since men and communities need faiths and values to live by. Distinct from this is the conflict between authoritative belief and the freedom of the individual to find in accordance with the evidence, which implies a form of self-discipline far from the attitude of indiscriminate skepticism. Only the discipline of following the evidence, exacting and laborious as it is, is the way to intellectual freedom. Indiscriminate skepticism goes with incapacity to follow the evidence, and is likely to create such intolerable mental and practical chaos that the victim finally seeks refuge in acceptance of some dogmatic authority. So indiscriminate and undisciplined skepticism is one way to the loss of freedom.

These various changing balances are all far-reaching and important, but clearly we cannot deal with them all here. We cannot here settle all the destinies of the world. But we may pick out a few high points on which an economist can have something to say.

3. THE WORLD IS INTERDEPENDENT

The world is interdependent, and this country is interdependent. It is an organic whole, a community. It is an imperfectly organized community, and perhaps it would be truer to say that it needs to become a community if it is to maintain its collective health and strength. No nation, no region, no part of a nation, can be fully sound if other important nations, or other parts of the same nation, are seriously sick. This is especially true of any nation devoted to peace, freedom and democracy. But I suspect that it has its applications, even in Soviet Russia. The Soviet government regards the noncommunist parts of the world as sick, and it appears to think that it cannot be fully sound until the rest of the world is cured of the sicknesses of capitalism and democratic socialism. It can quarantine itself against the contagions from outside—and also against any unbiased evidence as to how real this outside sickness is, so it pays a terrible and dangerous price in ignorance and mis-representation of the facts about the outside world. It can do all this with considerable success; but it is not satisfied with this quarantined status. It wants freedom of international intercourse, without exposure to this contagion: hence a sovietized world. We have different ideas. We think Russia is sick, but not because it has a different economic system from ours. The only Russian sickness we feel as a direct threat to us is precisely its conviction that a different economic system from its own *is* a sickness, and that the health of the world requires its forcible removal. But enough of that.

Both countries have their internal sicknesses, and for these also Russia uses the method of quarantine, plus sheer police repres-sion. These methods are in themselves a sickness, but one that is not to be cured quickly, or by any forcible action we can take. Our intervention after the Bolshevik revolution of 1917 should have taught us that. Perhaps Russia can quarantine itself, by means of slave labor camps, against the millions it appears to distrust. One suspects that this cannot be permanently successful, but while the centralized despotism holds sway, it may be conscious of no ill effects. A democracy is different. We cannot have a full feeling of health while the backwash of slavery condemns one racial group to a suppressed status, or while the sharecropper, or the south as a section, is economically handicapped, becoming a blighted sector of the community.

This does not imply that no one should ever have to face hard-ship or difficult conditions. That would be a stupid perversion of the idea that people should not have to grow up in unfavorable environments. In fact, one kind of unfavorable environment is that in which everything has been made too easy, and the indi-vidual has not been forced to develop his capacities for meeting real difficulties. That is not a kind of handicap from which a large proportion of the population are likely to suffer, though the ones who do, are likely to be among those with a high degree of innate capacity, so that unfavorable conditions for them are wasteful of good social material. Larger numbers suffer from the opposite extreme: conditions so hard that only a few can overcome them or escape from them, and the majority are doomed to defeat and frustration. Such conditions, whether in city slums, mining camps or sharecroppers' holdings, are a matter of community interest, not to abolish struggle, but to improve the conditions under which it goes on, to a point which permits the normal family, making good use of its capacities, to have hope of achieving an existence that has human meaning and content, beyond bare physical survival.

Modern conditions have split what should be a community into noncommunicating sectors: Park Avenue, Southampton, Hollywood, the lumber camp, the coal-mining town, the steel town, the camp of migratory harvest workers and Tobacco Road. A local community should ideally contain all the different groups which these place-names typify, within sight and knowledge of one another, so that King Wenceslaus may look out of his window and see the peasant gathering firewood in the snow, and respond as his nature may dictate. Where this natural contact is broken, there is need for some deliberate institutional devices to make up for what is lost.

One of the great sicknesses of the modern Great Society is that the constituent groups are separated not only physically but intellectually. Your world consists of what you hear and read, perhaps more fundamentally than what you see and touch; which means that people may live in the same apartment house, and yet inhabit separate and antagonistic worlds. Imagine, for example, seven people, one of whom gets his key picture of the world from the Wall Street Journal, one from the New York Times, one from the Chicago Tribune, one from the Nation, one from a farm journal, one from the Daily Worker and one from a sample of the Negro publications that circulate in Harlem. One of the alleviating features of the movies, partially compensating for a multitude of things that need alleviation, is their potentiality—only partially realized—for bridging these gulfs with a common medium. If their capacities were utilized, they could do much to make us into a community, and enable the parts to understand one another, instead of picturing one another in hackneyed and superficial stereotypes. I may seem to be wandering from a strictly economic theme, but I really am not, for such mutual understanding is one of the first requisites of sound community policy in economic matters. And all the agencies that are helping to bridge these gulfs are working for sound economic prosperity.

Decentralization of population and industry is good as a sheer physical matter of breaking up overgrown cities; but in social terms it might help or hinder, according as it was so handled as to build true community units of smaller size, or merely to move the existing truncated fractions farther apart, increasing the distance that separates absentee owners from the hired men who act as local managers of the decentralized industries. Decentralization needs to be guided by people who understand what a community is, and how important it is to maintain it.

4. A "FAVORABLE ECONOMIC CLIMATE" AS A BALANCED AFFAIR

One phase of the balance between business and government has been expressed in the appeal of business that government establish a "favorable climate" in which business may do its job. This has already been mentioned, indicating that it contains much truth, but is properly a two-sided affair.[1] The climate government sets for business is not the only important climatic condition for the economy. Government, as well as business, has a necessary and delicately difficult job to do in promoting a stable economy. It needs a favorable climate to succeed; and a major part of such a climate consists of the attitudes of business toward the policies government is forced to follow, including some that have an unavoidable experimental quality that might well cause uneasiness,

[1] See above, Chapter IV, pp. 112–13.

unless business has an underlying confidence, both in government and in its own capacity to adjust to novel policies. Business is not called on to forego the right of vigorous criticism of unsound policies, but it is called on to recognize the necessity of policies that explore outside the beaten tracks, and to do its best to meet such policies half way.

We have already noted that workable collective bargaining calls for recognition by each side that the other has a necessary job, and understanding of what it needs in order to do the job. This is also true of the relation between business and government. With this recognition and understanding as a basis, confidence can grow. Business needs to have confidence that government will not experiment capriciously, but only where a real need exists, and that it will be prudent and temperate, without letting itself be paralyzed by timidity. Such confidence needs to be earned by government, and business needs to give government a fair chance to earn it, and to be ready to accord it if it is earned, recognizing that it is not fair to expect either government or business to be infallible.

In order to be in a position to adopt an attitude that may earn this confidence, government needs to have confidence that business in general is meeting its responsibilities, and such confidence needs to be earned by business. It is an endless chain, which may become a vicious circle or a cumulative cycle of improved relations. The Committee for Economic Development has done much toward breaking the vicious circle, not only by proving that business can promote ends in harmony with community interest, but by promoting the growth among business men of a more understanding and hospitable attitude toward the part government has to play.

Perhaps the first step toward confidence in the face of things one does not like is simple understanding of their necessity. In the depression of the thirties, business was aghast at the mounting government deficits and full of apprehensions about them, which probably made its recovery less prompt and vigorous than it might have been. Then came the war, bringing vastly greater deficits, and business took them in its stride. This was, of course, due to a complex of reasons; it was partly because the deficits were conceived as temporary, but mainly because business accepted their necessity in an emergency which all were united to meet. So far, the emergencies of peace have not succeeded in rousing this spirit to anything like the same extent. If exploratory policies for sustaining employment can be met with a little of the same sense of emergency requiring united action, the resulting "favorable climate" might go far to make the difference between success and failure.

On the side of government, one of the greatest difficulties arises from superimposing one kind of control on another of a different sort. In the latter part of the nineteenth century, government began the piecemeal control of numerous specific abuses of business, thus developing an attitude of opposition to many business practices. Then, while continuing these piecemeal controls, it undertook also to combat depression, a task of a different sort, involving comprehensive policies of stimulation of business as a whole and requiring a more cooperative attitude. The morale engendered by one set of policies is an obstacle to the other.

Government consists of many agencies, each under an urge to correct any major defect in its own field. But there has been no agency whose business it was to decide how many defects it was practicable to try to correct at once. Government's left hand does not know too well what its right hand is doing; and in the past no one except the business man on the receiving end of the policies of control has had a picture of the total impact of all these controls on his sector of the economy. There is need for such a picture, somewhere in the agencies of government, which may give the whole program a more unified sense of proportion, and may help to decide whether the total of restrictive controls is consistent with a vigorous enterprising spirit and a strong constructive response to policies aimed at stimulation. It may be that the President's Council of Economic Advisers will constitute a large step toward filling this need.

5. BALANCE BETWEEN "PLANNING" AND FREEDOM

"Planning" in the most literal sense requires that someone have the power to execute the plan—to control individual actions in accord with it—else it is in danger of degenerating into a pious wish. And such changes of social balance as we face require intelligent foresight and measures aimed at an end result that someone consciously conceives. But the kind of planning that is consistent with freedom does not direct each industry what to produce and how many workers to employ. It deals with incentives, facilities and conditions, under which individual action may be influenced toward the goal without being coerced. Examples would be found among the policies affecting total expenditures, already discussed.

Sometimes the line gets rather thin which separates incentives and facilitating conditions from specific direction. But the Tennessee Valley Authority is an example of a successful adjustment of this sort, performing a distinguished task of stimulating a healthy, home grown economic development in a handicapped area of the country. This did not happen automatically; it happened because those in charge kept this goal continually in mind, and followed well-devised policies to this end, resisting the temptations to centralized and "bureaucratic" control. Industries must understand the goals of planning and, within the limits of their discretion and capacity, must work in general harmony with them. This is the great social experiment on which depends the success of our system in its task of adapting itself by evolution and avoiding revolution.

6. BALANCE BETWEEN SELF-INTEREST AND COLLECTIVE MOTIVES

In a changing balance between self-interest and collective motives, we come to the most basic of the "uncommon requirements" which our age lays upon the common man, if this is to be his century. James H. Breasted has spoken of the "age of character." Something of the sort has become a necessity if civilization is to survive. Politicians must become statesmen, as they sometimes do under pressure of emergency. Voters must support statesmanlike policies, as they often do if given strong leadership. And—hardest of all, perhaps—men in their everyday dealings must conduct them with an eye to their collective consequences. To repeat what seems to be the most crucial of economic principles for the age we face, the amount of liberty that can survive is dependent on, and measured by, the degree of responsibility with which economic power is exercised.

If we succeed, history will record that we rose to national greatness in the face of an emergency which threatened to overwhelm us. If we fail, there may be no history left, or none of the sort that we recognize, because it will be written in terms of a dictated "ideology," which substitutes authoritarian dogmas for the evidence of facts. Lest the magnitude of the task discourage us, we may console ourselves with the thought that a people can rise to greatness in this way, though most of them remain ordinary folks. They can do it if they have leadership, and the capacity to respond to it. Britain did it in the last war, though it was far from being made up, as Hitler exclaimed in 1940, of "forty-two million Churchills." There was defeatism, there were many who would have yielded under the strain; but the nation did not yield. And we may find, in 1955 or 1960, that we have done it, though we are far from being one hundred and forty-five million saints, heroes or social geniuses.

We need better people. Do we need to breed them, biologically? At present, we do not know enough of the laws of heredity for that —fortunately or unfortunately. Lacking that, much depends on the process called education. President Butler of Columbia once called America the "best half-educated nation in the world." For what we face today a half-educated people is not good enough. Formal education has its limitations, as students are aware. It has a deplorable way of stopping when the student leaves the campus, just when some of the most crucial parts of his education begin. Learning needs to be a lifelong process, in which the things one learned in one's formal schooling are adjusted to reality, not abandoned in face of it. It needs to equip the student with adaptable mental tools, not with a completed single-purpose intellectual machine. And it needs to afford him exercise in the flexible, but disciplined, use of the tools. Above all, it needs to build well-balanced personalities to maintain poise and judgment in face of the changing balances we have been looking at.

We have to choose to follow a code of social morality, and to build the code, though free to do otherwise as men have never been free before. This test has probably never been faced as fully as now, when the free and intellectually emancipated peoples are confronted with the necessity of working out an altered scheme of self-discipline, in the absence of authority that can discipline them from above.

We need to do generous, constructive thinking in the face of terrifying danger, and that takes more than intellect. We need to face ugly facts—to be ruthless with ourselves in that one respect—and still hold fast to ideals and to good will, and resist all temptation to think that material ruthlessness toward others, here and now, is a sound road through present perplexities to some millennial end. That way lies the threat of totalitarianism, which might conquer us from within if not from without. The task calls for the most difficult exercise of discriminating judgment. In the words of Gordon Keith Chalmers: "To know (these temptations and these enemies), to know the fine shade of right which marks it from a similar shade of wrong, to know when pride turns virtue into vice, when sacrifice becomes vainglory, when ideals become hypocrisy—this knowledge requires the most manly skill and courage available to men." This is the highest task of education.

[1] From "A New View of the World," in *The Humanities After the War*, p. 79.

7. ECONOMIC FORMULAS VERSUS DEMOCRATIC SOLUTIONS

This country wants to solve its problems democratically, and democratic solutions must grow, not be imposed. This means that no one can prescribe a program for the whole structure of society. No one executive, no lawmaker, no builder of theoretical economic models and certainly no lecturer on a platform can do this. These all have their place, but all proposals are ideas that go into the great hopper, to rub their corners off against other ideas and perhaps, if they have worth, to come out in altered forms and combinations. One of the besetting fallacies of reformers is the delusion that their plans will be carried out by people who think precisely as they do. And the beginning of democratic wisdom is to realize that they will not, and to frame them accordingly, to be carried out with the participation of other people, and to be modified in the process.

It is in that spirit that I have been expressing my ideas here; otherwise I should be guilty of intolerable presumption. Economists have an increasingly important place in our social scheme, but it remains a limited one. They are specialists in certain kinds of relationships of cause and effect which enter into the behavior of our system, but are far from being the whole of it. Some of these relationships have the finality of mathematics; and it is natural for an economist to emphasize these, since they represent the problems to which he can furnish precise answers. For example, if some forms of expenditure increase, some of the consequences are definitely calculable; and such calculations can be increasingly valuable, as economic science makes progress in working out their implications. But we have seen that many of the most important consequences depend on how people will respond; and people are free to respond in various ways, according to their changing habits and understanding, their attitudes and moods.

From the record of human behavior we can chart past responses, and so learn a good deal about probable future ones, especially the ones that show a great deal of stability. Some of these charts are in statistical form, and most of them have consequences that are susceptible of statistical measurement. Statistics are ponderous and unwieldy, though they may become less so with the development of methods which make small samples more reliable bases for inference, and make it possible to learn useful things about the more detailed and particular reactions of the parts of the system, and to keep the information closer to the current frontier where things are changing. A complementary kind of study, harder to achieve, probes into the motives and attitudes that lie behind the statistical record, and explain why people respond as they do. As progress is made in this field of inquiry, it may become more nearly possible to forecast, tentatively, how responses are likely to change with changing conditions.

All these kinds of study have their place. Even lectures have their place, though the world cannot be saved by giving lectures, nor by listening to them. What counts is the further creative process of putting ideas into action. If one had the correct formula to meet conditions as they are in the winter of 1947-8, by the time a series of lectures can appear in print, some features of the situation will have changed; and by the time you who are listening are actively grappling with these problems, the front will have moved on. It would be a bold man who could be confident as to what parts of these lectures, if any, would retain their pertinence. You have been listening patiently to these discussions, including much that you know already, and some tentative gropings for ideas that might usefully animate the next steps we shall have to take. I believe some of these ideas are sound, but I cannot prove it as a physicist is accustomed to prove his results.

The ideas go into the hopper, with the hope that they include some useful ingredients, and may not be all waste material when the vast machine has done its grinding and the product comes out at the other end. I had almost said "the final product"; but no products of this mill are final. The result cannot be guaranteed, and if it is successful, what is gained is chiefly a chance to go on working at the next set of problems. Democracy is living dangerously, and if it is saved today it must be saved again tomorrow. But if most of us do our part, there is a fair fighting chance that the country may emerge from the peculiarly testing decades that are ahead, as a basically sound and workable economic community.

I N D E X

Acton, Lord, quoted, 61
Agrarian reform, 10, 24, 29, 43
Agrarian collectivization, 24, 29
Agricultural price supports, 119. See also Prices, sensitive and insensitive
Alliance for collective defense, 35–36
Annual wage, 98, 155–157
Antitrust policy, 143, 185
Appeasement, 3, 33–35, 40
Arbitration of labor disputes, 187
Archangel expedition, 8, 38 n.
Atom bomb, 3–4, 12, 35, 53

Balance of power, 188
Bastiat, 12
Benes, 11 n.
Bentham, 68 n., 181
Bergson, Abram, cited, 16 n.
Beveridge, Lord, cited, 77, 98, 155
Blitzkrieg, 17–18
Bolshevik revolution of 1917, 7–8, 38, 194
Booms, 99. See also Fluctuations
Breasted, James H., 200
Bulganin, 38
Bulk-line cost studies, 144
Business cycles, 156. See also Booms; Depressions; Fluctuations; Recessions
Butler, President, 200
Byrnes, James A., 46

Capital, 157, 159
Capital goods, 83, 137–38
Capital outlays, 85–7, 91–4, 96–7, 99–103, 105–106, 111–12, 132–133, 135, 137–139, 165–168, 176; autonomous vs. derived, 167; labor-saving, 161–162, 167–168; restraint on, 99; stabilization by contract, 101, 139–140, 143
Capitalism, 12, 13, 42, 44, 63. See also Private enterprise
Cartels, 140
Cash balances, 129–30. See also Money
Catholic church, 57
Centralia mine disaster, 49
Chalmers, Gordon Keith, quoted, 201
Character, age of, 62, 200
Clark, John Bates, 59
Class war, 7
Classes, 15, 17; changing alignment of, 189–190
Climate, favorable, for business, 112–113, 196–198
Cobb, C. W., cited, 158 n.
Collective bargaining, 147–163, 169–170, 178–188, 197; enlightened self-interest in, 181–182; mature attitudes in, 179, 186–187; need of, 60; politics of, 179–182
Collectivism, 44, 45, 71; and collective bargaining, 147; danger to democracy, 64; distinguished from totalitarianism, 6; English, 29; and full employment, 55. See also Socialism
Comintern and Cominform, 18
Committee for Economic Development, 197
Communism, 6–7, 192. See also Marxism, Soviet Russia
Communist party, 46

205